Stephen Spender · David Hockney

China Diary

Harry N. Abrams, Inc., Publishers, New York

To Gregory Evans
who helped us on our journey

The photographs on pp. 8, 29 and 41 (below) were
taken by Stephen Spender, and those on pp. 71, 105 and
107 (top) by Gregory Evans; all the other illustrations
are by David Hockney, with the exception of the map
on p. 6, specially drawn by Hanni Bailey.

The authors and publisher wish to express their
gratitude to David Graves of Petersburg Press, London,
for his valuable help in the realization of this project.

Library of Congress Cataloging in Publication Data

Spender, Stephen, 1909–
  China diary.

  1. China—Description and travel—1976–
2. Spender, Stephen, 1909– —Journeys—China.
3. Authors, English—20th century—Biography.
I. Hockney, David. II. Title.
DS712.S65 1983   915.1′0458   82–8783
ISBN 0-8109-0783-6   AACR2

© 1982 Stephen Spender and David Hockney

Filmset in Great Britain by Tameside Filmsetting Ltd, Ashton under Lyne
Monochrome origination in Great Britain by DCSI, London
Color origination in Switzerland by Cliché Lux, Neuchâtel
Printed in the Netherlands by Smeets B.V., Weert
Bound in the Netherlands by Van Rijmenam, The Hague

Contents

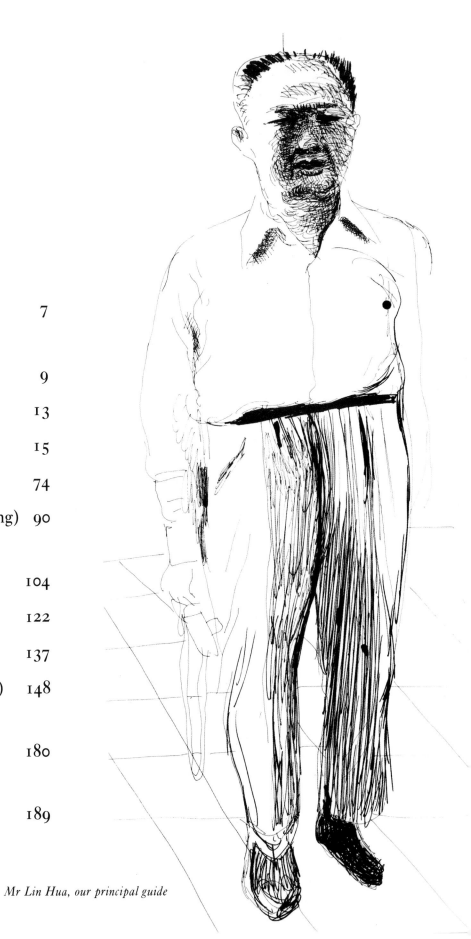

Mr Lin Hua, our principal guide

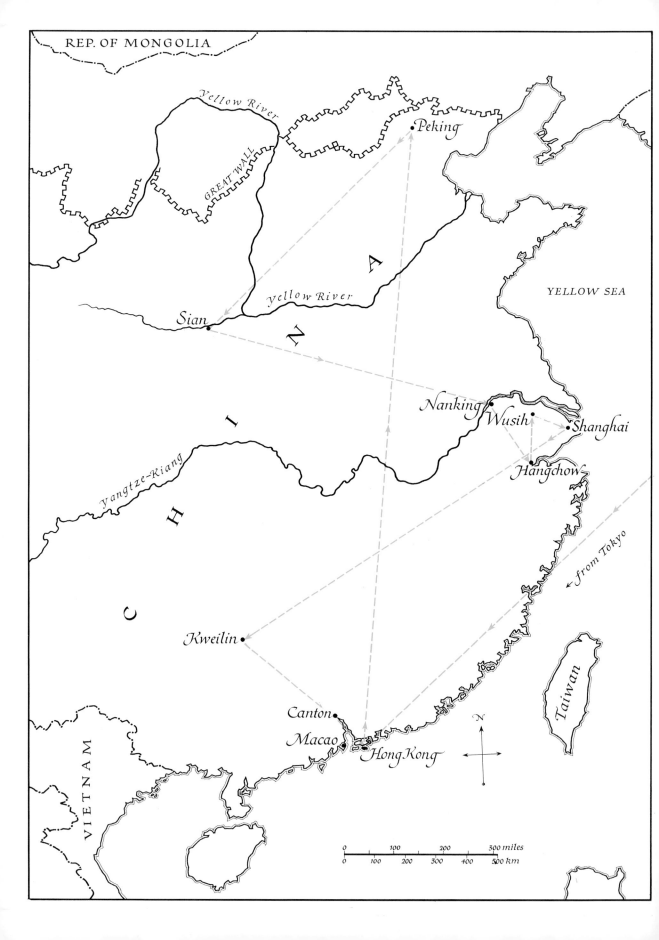

Prologue

avid Hockney, his assistant Gregory Evans and I left Los Angeles on Tuesday, 19 May 1981. On the evening of the 18th we had dined at Lawry's restaurant, famous for its roast beef. The film director Tony Richardson who was with us talked about a tour he had made in China. He said he refused to follow the instructions of the guide of his group, leaving the other members of it and going by himself wherever he liked. He recommended us to do likewise.

We had known for over a year that we were going to make this trip, but in the autumn of 1980 we had to postpone it because David was taken up with designing sets for a programme of two one-act operas and one ballet for the Metropolitan Opera in New York – Francis Poulenc's *Les Mamelles de Tirésias*, Erik Satie's short ballet *Parade* and Maurice Ravel's *L'Enfant et les Sortilèges*. So great was the success of this programme that we almost had to postpone going once more because the Metropolitan Opera had given him a further commission to do sets for three short Stravinsky works – *Le Rossignol, Sacre du Printemps* and *Oedipus Rex*.

This is David Hockney's book – as well as mine – for his paintings, drawings and photographs illustrate the pages that follow, and I also include many of the things he said on our travels. Eight months after our return from China we met again in Los Angeles; looking through all the material, we recalled and discussed the salient features of our journey. Extracts from these conversations – largely David's memories and ideas for the eventual form of the book – appear at the end as an Epilogue. On that occasion he proposed: 'Let's begin by saying it's just a little personal trip we made together. I think the book should be in that sense a bit bitty – like life – patched up in some way, as if made by three schoolboys on a tour of a continent for the first time. I think that's the only way it will work.'

Spellings of Chinese names
Although the use of the Pinyin system is now official, we have preferred in this book to retain the more familiar Wade-Giles transliteration, with the Pinyin equivalent given in parentheses at the first mention of the names of the main centres visited.

DH by SS

GE by SS

SS by DH

China Diary

19 May

On the day of our departure from Los Angeles David and Gregory fetched me from the Tropicana Motel, where I was staying, and together we drove to the airport. On reaching this vast confused area of concrete and glass, we soon found ourselves in the departure lounge awaiting our flight which was due to take off at 12.00 noon; the first leg, to Tokyo, would take ten hours, then – after a two-hour stop spent in the transit lounge – the second leg, of about five hours, would take us on to Hong Kong. Seated facing a desk with two airline officials behind it were our fellow-passengers, among whom were square-jawed, box-templed Japanese businessmen wearing black oblong horn-rimmed spectacles, American tourists with expressions of eager anticipation, and Chinese bringing from the corrupt West presents to their families.

The China International Travel Service, the mysterious power which had spent at least six months pondering the conditions of our journey, had decided to send us by way of Tokyo and Hong Kong, perhaps because the less frequent direct flights from Tokyo to Peking were already booked, perhaps because some official had decided that we should have the opportunity of comparing the corruption of the British Colony with the purity of the Chinese People's Republic (we were to discover later that a lot of thought had been given to planning our schedule).

I had with me on the aeroplane three or four books about China and, sitting immediately behind David and Gregory, I intermittently read these. David had with him a portable tape recorder and occasionally he would put on headphones and transfer himself as if on a magic carpet of sound back to the Metropolitan Opera performances of *L'Enfant et les Sortilèges* a year ago or forward to *Le Rossignol* to be given six months hence. At intervals throughout the three-week period of our journey he would take these trips back and forth in time and place, for our visit to China was only a hiatus between places conditioning our lives in the West.

David wore a white flat peaked cap and a striped jersey, Gregory a yellow Robin-Hoodish kind of jerkin, canary-coloured, I a fawn-coloured camel-hair jacket and dark-blue trousers. David, from the intensity of looking through his gold-rimmed spectacles, has, when drawing or taking photographs, a pursed-up expression, his features focusing on some target of his attention. Gregory resembles one of the group of young Florentine nobles standing in the foreground of Botticelli's *Adoration of the Magi*. David always had with him two Pentax cameras, one a lightweight 35-mm model for black and white, the other a 110 model for colour. I had a 35-mm Olympus 2. David had also a Polaroid camera (Tony Richardson had told us that the Chinese loved nothing more than Polaroid photographs of themselves – and this certainly proved true).

While we were sitting in the transit lounge at Tokyo airport, David did a drawing of me looking saturated with exhaustion like a sponge with water. After living with myself for over seventy years I have, I suppose, a kind of serial image of myself though it is unlikely that one will recognize oneself in the final emanation of the series. The general impression I made in David's drawing was of bulbous obesity: bulbous cheeks, chins, limbs and fingers. Later drawings in wash or crayon confirmed an overall redness rendered sheep-like by the whitest of woollen hair. The eyes are veined pink by eye-strain. With the retina of one eye distorting lines it sees – or doesn't see – into curves, and with knees creaking after an accident two years ago in which I severed the ligaments of both knees and had them sewn up – and with my considerable height and overall largeness I must have looked very much

SS at Tokyo airport

the odd man out compared with my two younger companions. It is obvious though that all three of us must have looked comical to the Chinese and this should be remembered because those observed are themselves observers of the observers and sometimes cannot prevent themselves laughing at them. We looked a bit absurd, especially me with my big feet.

During the second leg of our flight, from Tokyo to Hong Kong, I continued reading. I was struck by a passage from Mao Tse-tung's speeches (cited in the anthology *China Yesterday and Today*) entitled 'On the People's Democratic Dictatorship'. Here is an extract:

'You are dictatorial.'
My dear sirs, what you say is correct. That is just what we are. All the experiences of the Chinese people, accumulated in the course of successive decades, tell us to carry out a people's democratic dictatorship. This means that the reactionaries must be deprived of the right to voice their opinions; only the people have that right.
Who are the 'people'? At the present stage in China, they are the working class, the peasantry, the petty bourgeoisie, and the national bourgeoisie.
Under the leadership of the working class and the Communist Party, these classes unite to create their own state and elect their own government so as to enforce their dictatorship over the henchmen of imperialism – the landlord class and bureaucratic capitalist class as well as the reactionary clique of the Kuomintang which represents those classes and their accomplices. The people's government will suppress such persons. It will only allow them to behave themselves properly. It will not allow them to speak or act wildly. Should they do so, they will be instantly curbed and punished. The democratic system is to be carried out within the ranks of the people, giving them freedom of speech, assembly and association. The right to vote is given only to the people, not the reactionaries.
These two things, democracy for the people, and dictatorship for the reactionaries, when combined, constitute the people's democratic dictatorship.

I thought that Mao Tse-tung's words were, from the standpoint of the time when he wrote them, irrefutable; with hindsight of today, entirely fallible.

But supposing that on that far yesterday in 1949 he had some prophetic ability to look back on himself with hindsight of thirty years later, they would still, for that time, have been irrefutable because the Chinese revolution could certainly never have been achieved without employing ruthless dictatorial methods and removing all opposition. I went on reading:

Why must things be done in this way? Everyone is very clear on this point. If things were not done like this, the revolution would fail, and people would suffer, and the state would perish.
'Don't you want to abolish state power?'
Yes, we want to but not at the present time. We cannot afford to abolish state power just now. Why not? Because imperialism still exists, because, internally, revolutionaries still exist and classes still exist.

Again, the first paragraph seems irrefutable. Again fallibility seems woven into the second. State power is to be abolished like sin but not just yet, dear Lord – never just yet. But the longer the state is dictatorial, the more difficult will it be to abolish tyranny. There is not anywhere a dictatorship under which some class of public servants is trained to run the government when the state withers away. There was, I thought, the Cultural Revolution in China but, although this resulted for a time in near anarchy, its purpose was not to destroy the centralized power of the state. From Mao Tse-tung's point of view, its purpose was, in the name of continual revolution, to reinstate the authority of Chairman Mao, who had been set aside as a mere figurehead by his colleagues and who had lost his basis of power.

Thoughts like these pursued me all the time we were in China even in my sleep, I think, for sometimes they took the form of nightmares. They were typical thoughts of someone of my generation. It seemed appropriate that they should start in the aeroplane because they were floating – *flottant* as the French say. They corresponded though to something that I felt to be floating in China itself where the current of life seems today liquescent, with all the fixed ideas of communism, Maoism, pragmatism, individualism, in a state of flux, all floated over by the balloon-like portraits of Chairman Mao on walls.

David, being of his generation and 44 as against my 72, does not have the same tendency to think along lines laid down by the history of power politics in this century. He used, he told me when we talked about this, at one time to vote Labour but today party politics don't interest him. This may be due in part to the fact that, from the point of view of an English painter who divides his life between Los Angeles and London, party politics seem parochial. He looks at life, he says, from the point of view of the imagination. The imagination is to him a kind of ultimate force directing – or which should direct – everything. Often he exclaims 'Everything is imagination', as though this thought were some touchstone in his mind. Science is there to provide the technological means whereby the imagined can be made real.

Once I mentioned to David that some French professor – a structuralist, I think – had said that we in the West could not possibly ever understand the Chinese because their whole way of thinking and patterns of behaviour conditioning them were outside the context of our way of thinking and the patterns of behaviour conditioning us. David was indignant: 'I could not believe that for one moment,' he said. 'To do so is to deny our common humanity.'

I suppose that one would have to describe David as an optimist, though myself I do not care for that word. It seems to indicate some kind of moral myopia, the opposite of the kind called pessimistic. It would be more to the point to say that he thinks it a virtue – almost a moral imperative – to regard life as a *donnée*, a condition given, to be enjoyed. He resents people doing life down. At any rate, he thinks that there's something to be got out of it for most people.

On our travels David and I were, I think, corrective to each other because I am able to point out to him that he should not expect everyone in the world to have his capacity for enjoyment; and he corrects in me the tendency to be got down or over-impressed by the sheer weight of seemingly insuperable obstacles and in-soluble problems, to live as it were under a dark vague cloud of uncomprehended and, I suspect, incomprehensible statistics. He had a glimpse of the insoluble negations of the world, which I seem mentally to inhabit much of the time, when he went to India. On our travels he said that, however bad things may be in China, they are worse in India.

David likes Los Angeles because he regards it as being in a perpetual state of transformation. Los Angeles tomorrow will not be the Los Angeles you dislike today, he says to friends who complain about L.A. On our trip he sometimes said that he thought America was nearer to communism than China with its bureaucrats, its stratification of the population into about thirty different classes, its top rulers moving around in cars looking like hearses and with side windows through which it is as difficult to see the top people as it is to see harems in the smoke-glass limousines of Arab sheiks. In China today officials live in apartments more hidden from the public gaze than those of any Emperor and his retinue in the Forbidden City.

20 May   Hong Kong

When we arrived at Hong Kong it was evening; we were, to our surprise, met by a dark-suited, sleek young Chinese who spirited us through customs and guided us to a Rolls-Royce in which we were driven to the Peninsula Hotel in Kowloon. We had large luxurious suites with doors padded on the outside with leather: inside-out padded cells for millionaires, I thought. In the bathroom, casketed in boxes that looked as if they were made of sandalwood (plastic really), were bars of soaps of five or six varieties, each one a gift from the management who had also had a bowl of exotic fruit placed on a table by my bed. The bed itself was king size. From his room, David dialled a call to Los Angeles and got through at once. We were not yet cut off from the outside world.

I contented myself with sampling, from my bowl of fruit, a paw-paw (I think it was that). Looking out across the harbour, I could see the lights of Hong Kong against the sky, like strips of black-and-white transparent developed photographic negative hanging on a wire, with stars above them. Lights wriggle like snakes in the water below. At this point we are all too exhausted to eat or go out tonight. Sleep.

21 May

This morning we feel energetic, alert, excited and everything we should be. We breakfast early at one of the marble tables in the great reverberating columned hotel hall. From here we can see stone-paved corridors with plate-glass shop-windows full of luxury goods. We go down a wide street at the side of the hotel. It has high buildings either side like any Main Street of a town in the American Mid-West. The side streets are more exciting with the spaces between houses sometimes so packed with signs that they look like advertising pages of newspapers pasted in sheets between houses. The letters are mostly Chinese characters but there are some signs in English. In these narrow streets every shop seems to sell either hi-fi, stereo equipment and tape cassettes, or cameras, or jewellery and watches – things the young yearn for in Canton, we are later to discover.

To me, the prices don't seem markedly different from anywhere else, but that is because I don't bargain. Apparently, the fun of Hong Kong is to go from shop to shop, finding where things are cheapest.

We return to the waterfront and walk back past our hotel and a domed hall opposite it which looks like an immense concrete mushroom, to the harbour ferry. David loves ferries, especially the Staten Island Ferry in New York, which – with the spectacular view of the Manhattan skyline that it affords passengers – he considered 'the most beautiful and by far the cheapest trip to be made in New York; but the view across the harbour at Hong Kong is even more beautiful', he says. In spitting rain we board the ferry with its benches on deck. We look at the skyscrapers on the other side of the harbour. Seen through rain forming a screen in front of them they seem like different-sized caryatids supporting marble cross-beams of clouds.

We disembark from the ferry and walk through the rain among Banks and Chambers of Commerce and rather grand stores. David darts into a shop and emerges with three stubby umbrellas for us. Gregory makes one of his laconic remarks with which he punctuates our trip: 'Money is what Hong Kong is about.'

We do not have time to savour any of Hong Kong's famous dishes because our flight to Peking leaves at 2 p.m. In fact, we have to hurry back on the ferry to our hotel, pack our bags and have them taken down to the lobby to be put back in the Rolls-Royce in which the same elegant young Chinese returns us to the airport as pompously as we were met on arrival. We have luncheon in the vast airport restaurant which is set back on a stagey platform above the reception area. From here we have a view over the airport, rainy beyond plate-glass walls and traversed by the ruled lines of the runways. Aeroplanes of all nations are scattered on its surface looking like ships in dry dock with their hulls exposed. Wings and fins form abstract patterns against the background of skyscrapers and an undulating mountain skyline in the far distance. Lettering and names on their fuselages look like addresses scrawled on aluminium envelopes.

At the restaurant we have a surprisingly good Chinese meal – far better than most of those we are to get in China. While we are eating, David asks me: 'Have I ever told you my theory of the effect of mechanical aids such as the *camera obscura* on Western art?' I say, no, and he goes on: 'Well, it seems to me that as the result of using the *camera obscura* Western artists tended to see nature not through their two eyes but through a single lens, accruing a great deal of irrelevant detail around the image.' While we talked I saw in my mind's eye a dome in Venice with a skylight through which rays of light spread downwards in an inverted V, projecting onto a marble table a view of the Grand Canal – exact in every detail as a drawing by Guardi or Canaletto. David said: 'Of course, I don't know whether Chinese painters had such mechanical aids but it seems to me that in their work they concentrated on the essential images as they saw them and eliminated unnecessary details. In the West artists have turned to Japanese or Chinese art because the painters there selected in their work the essentials.'

When we boarded the Chinese Airways (CAAC) plane it seemed like a school bus in comparison with the Boeing 747 we had been in before. Seats were close together, the gangway narrow. It was full of American tourists, women for the most part. Shepherding this flock was a tall, smiling Chinese guide. He was instructing the Americans how to fill in forms for customs. In his black suit and black-rimmed glasses he had the look of a young priest as he walked down the aisle receiving admiring glances from rows of lady passengers. These American tourists seemed all set on loving China and atoning for the years of division which – until Nixon's visit in 1972 – had poisoned Sino-American relations. To many Americans, China is a love-object, once tended by American missionaries, teachers and doctors, many of whom spent their lives in Chinese villages or slums and worked to help the people there. These Americans were grieved by the quarrel with the Chinese People's Republic, beginning with America's support of Chiang Kai-shek after the Second World War and continuing through the Korean War and the war in Vietnam. Was Nixon responding to some deep emotion in the hearts of such Americans, Christian believers in good works, when he went to China in 1972 and healed the breach between the two countries? Perhaps this will be seen to be the best thing Nixon did and one of the sincerest: fulfilling some impulse of his own Quaker upbringing. There is something simple, innocent and smiling about the Chinese, especially in the countryside, which awakens a chord of response in the minds of American Christians, Quakers, Baptists, pacifists, scholars and purists or puritans. Not to be scoffed at.

Peking (Beijing)

When we arrived at Peking airport it seemed so small I still cannot quite believe it. There must be more airports, I thought, and learned later that there is also a military airport and another for domestic flights.

The reception area seemed equally modest. While we stood in the arrival and customs hall looking at the railings which divided us from the real China beyond the neutral world of passports, what appeared to be the only conveyor belt for luggage had stuck. One or two porters in blue dungarees dived through the hatch to fish out our bags. They were remarkably quick about it.

Any airport one arrives at seems to strike the note of that place in relation to the places one has left. Here was Peking, so unpretentious: provincial seeming (in terms of the West), totally without the advertising display which is the fortissimo opening chord of the airports of great cities in capitalist countries. Nowhere could seem on arrival less powerful than China. How could it be one of the world's super-powers?, I was already asking myself. Why were the Russians terrified of it?

As soon as we got through customs, which we seemed to do like lightning, we were met by our two guides, Mr Lin Hua – who for the next three weeks was to Virgil to our threesome Dante – and Miss Li. Mr Lin was rotund, smiling with commanding intelligent features – so there was some affinity in his appearance to those photographs of Mao Tse-tung which one sees everywhere in China – as though we had a miniature Great Helmsman as our guide. Mr Lin certainly extolled the merits of Chairman Mao on every possible occasion – emphasizing particularly his pre-eminence as poet, scholar, calligrapher, philosopher. Miss Li – who was only to be with us during our stay in Peking – had features that looked prettily carved from wood and varnished a kind of transparent brown like the scroll of a 'cello.

This was to be the pattern of our tour: Mr Lin always with us and every place we went a local guide who sprang up on our arrival, usually scared stiff, not so much of us, we thought, as of Mr Lin, whom we took to be an important official and whose character became one of our chief topics of conversation at meals in the evening when we were usually by ourselves.

Up till now, we had not the faintest idea how we would be received in China. We rather assumed, despite our London publishing sponsor's previous assurances, that we would tag along with the Americans who had been with us on the plane – or some similar group of tourists. So it was with bounding relief that we found ourselves being conducted to a minibus just for ourselves: and with a smug sense of superiority as we got into it, we saw our fellow-passengers being herded into a huge charabanc.

In anticipation of our being three out of a crowd of thirty or so, David had tried to raise our spirits: 'Remember that the tourists looking at things are just as interesting as the things they are looking . . .', and he recalled 'When I went to Egypt I was one of a group of tourists and, after a bit, I found them just as interesting as the antiquities. . . .'

We were hurried to our minibus, our luggage with us. Mr Lin told us we were in a great hurry. We were to dine with the British Council's Peking Representative in half an hour. The minibus was Japanese – a Toyota; it was air-conditioned and had ten seats. A considerable part of our life was spent in it during the next five days. We came to regard it with affection as a kind of home from home. David and Gregory usually sat in the front seats, and I by the doorway where there was room to stretch my legs. Mr Lin, with Miss Li beside him, occupied the space between us, providing us with information of a general and principled nature which Miss Li filled out with local statistics (such mundane matters seemed perhaps beneath the attention of Mr Lin).

David did a schematic drawing of the drive from the airport along a straight road with straight rows of trees on either side. Beyond the trees, of which there were sometimes as many as six rows, there were fields – all very flat and very green. The road finally became an avenue with blocks of high tenement buildings either side. I asked our local guide what these were: 'Housing for the people,' she said, and

The drive from the airport

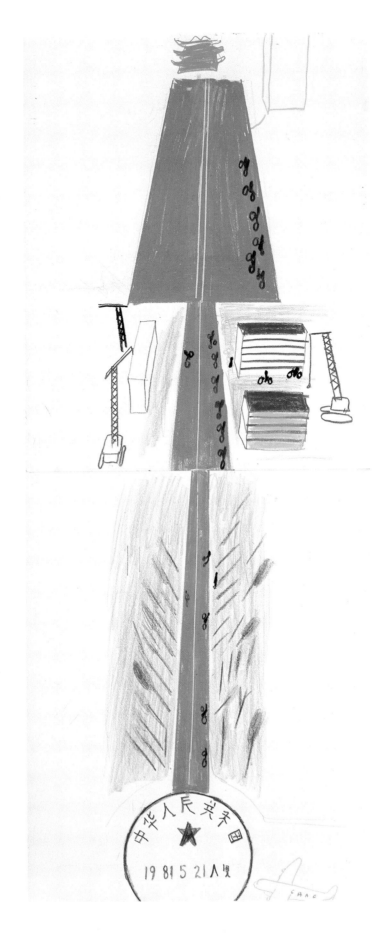

added that had it not been for the subversive activities of the Gang of Four, there would be many more such tenements.

This was the first time we heard mention of Those who are Guilty for Everything that is Wrong – the thought of them caused the gentle Miss Li's voice to tremble and her face to redden. It was like the harsh vibrations on the drums in the orchestra accompanying a Chinese opera when the dragon-villain appears.

I asked what people were housed in the tenements, and she explained that occupiers were decided on according to priorities. I remarked on the great number of cyclists in the streets as we approached the city. 'Three million of the nine million inhabitants of Peking have bicycles,' she told us with a bright smile.

At breakfast the next morning David and Gregory worried about this. How did the six million people without bicycles get along? 'Well, some would be too young, others too old to need bicycles,' I said, 'and in a family one bicycle might conveniently be used by two people.' David later discovered, by going to bicycle shops, that a bicycle cost 150 yuan and that the average monthly wage of a worker was 100 yuan. He also pointed out that all bicycles were padlocked, which seemed to contradict what we had been told by Miss Li, that no one in China ever stole. Not that we had any expectation that all the Chinese would be saints. It was only our being told how perfectly honest they were that drew attention to the matter. And, of course, nothing was stolen from any of us at any time there – the property of foreign visitors is meticulously guarded. It was curious to read in the newspapers when we got home that in the spring of 1981 China was said to be in the middle of a crime wave.

As we saw it then, driving in from the airport, Peking seemed to consist of vast grey dusty vague areas with broken walls that merge into houses, roads that seem to lead into roads being laid down (they are tearing up sections of the city to extend the underground railway). We had an impressionless impression which gave us the feeling that we were minute dots or crosses on an aerial photograph of a partly bombed out city which, in some areas, was undergoing reconstruction. We scarcely had time to put our things down in the hall of the Peking Hotel, before we were rushed off again in our minibus to meet the British Council Representative and his wife, Mr and Mrs Keith Hunter, at the Kau Ru Ji restaurant with tables outside on a balcony overlooking a part of the lake, Shi Sha Hai, the main expanse of which could be seen further off. With boys and girls dressed mostly in blue and walking by the lakeside and looking out across the water, the scene was like some pastel of working-class Parisians on the banks of the Seine done in the early part of the century; except that the boys and girls did not embrace or hold hands. Or that is how I saw it. (To judge from his later comments – see Epilogue – David clearly didn't have the same impression.)

After dinner we went back to the Hunters' apartment which was large and English, with armchairs and sofas and pictures of English scenes on the walls. Mrs Hunter showed us examples of bonsai trees which she was growing. She explained how by cramping the roots you torture a plant into dwarfitude. David stretched himself out exhausted in an armchair – or did he lie on the floor? Mrs Hunter – who had a pleasantly teasing manner – sometimes addressed me as 'professor' or 'my hero' – alluded to the fact that David was wearing one blue and one canary-yellow sock. David said yes, when he was twelve years old, and living at his parents' home in Bradford, he read Robert Herrick's poem 'Delight in Disorder':

> *A sweet disorder in the dress*
> *Kindles in clothes a wantonness:*
>
> *. . .*
>
> *A careless shoe-string, in whose tie*
> *I see a wild civility:*
> *Do more bewitch me than when art*
> *Is too precise in every part.*

He said that when he first read these lines he had thought, 'Well, that's perfectly true, there must be something good about poetry if poets say things like that', and continued to read poetry ever after while exemplifying in his attire Herrick's lines. He also recited two poems by Walter Raleigh.

Later, David recalled that during our first days in Peking he didn't take many photographs. He had thought he would be able to make drawings and indeed did make a few of the great avenue – the Avenue of Perpetual Peace – in front of the brick-and-concrete mass of the Peking Hotel, with room for perhaps twelve lanes of traffic ('but the traffic explosion hasn't yet begun', he remarked), of Tian An Men Square, a vast empty parade ground with the long red walls of the Imperial City, and the Gate of Heavenly Peace (the Tian An Men), the Monument to the People's Heroes and the Mao Tse-tung Memorial Hall. Then he started taking more and more photographs. He took photographs of the crimson wall, peeling in

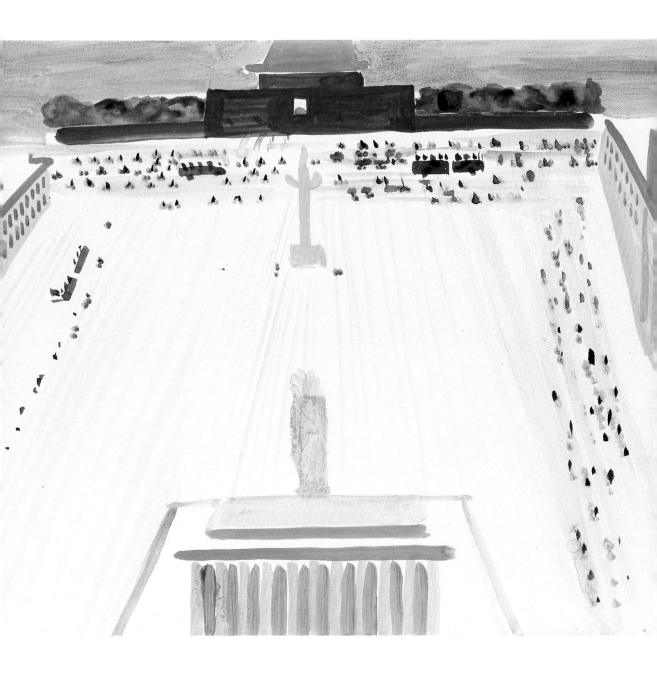

Tian An Men Square

places and with graffiti, and with Gregory leaning against it, at the back of the Forbidden City where Gregory and he went one morning before breakfast. David's camera took in everything. He and Gregory noticed that the TV in their hotel room wouldn't work, the reason being that the plug didn't fit into the socket. So he photographed the set and the adjacent socket. In the course of our trip, because of our hectic schedule (getting up early, sometimes at six, and seeing things till eight at night), photographing became more and more necessary. 'Here is the little old lady with bandaged feet (I didn't dare take a photograph of the whole lady)', he said as we went through the photographs afterwards. 'Here is a little perambulator which looks like a bird-cage, and the baby in it like a chicken.' 'Here is a radiogram in a shop window in Sian that really looks as though it was designed in about 1940 in America.' 'Here is another shop window with two vacuum cleaners and three electric fans in it.' 'Here is a shop window of a photographer's with portrait photographs in the window.' 'Here is one of me trying to make a drawing in Sian.' 'Bicycles, bicycles and bicycles.'

Later, in Los Angeles, he recalled that he fell back on using the camera to record people, architecture and little details: 'It wasn't easy to be a journalistic artist, I found. Also I began to be a little more conscious of the need to take them more carefully. The problem of going to a place and taking photographs is this: you are looking through a frame, seeing separate pictures framed up, peripheral vision stops. You don't see everything if you take photographs. It's a paradox.'

Shop-window displays

The Peking Hotel, seventeen storeys high, and built in the Soviet unimaginitive utilitarian style, is reserved for foreign tourists and official guests. Taxi-drivers hang about outside the portico waiting for fares. The ground floor has an immense lobby, always full of in-going and out-going guests, and their luggage, always handled with the greatest efficiency and honesty. Shops selling souvenirs and other things lead off this lobby. Upstairs there are banqueting rooms and a large dining room, as utilitarian in design as the rest. In the dining room we have a small table for four only, at one end, from which we can see in the distance tables for distinguished guests of the State, one of whom, during our stay, was Mr David Rockefeller, the U.S. banker.

From my room on the fifth floor I have a view every morning of people doing exercises in a courtyard some blocks from the hotel. I think it must be a military establishment because there are installations for doing rather elaborate exercises. But it may not be. Doing exercises in China is a more widespread and more diverse activity than jogging in America. Whatever communism does to the mind, it does achieve in China what might be called the democracy of bodies. Everyone seems to regard his or her physique as an instrument to be improved not just for his or her sake but as an organ of the body of the whole community. In this respect the Chinese nation votes with its muscles.

Mr Lin and Miss Li

Mr Lin is quite the disciplinarian. He tells us when we should appear in the lobby; and outdoors when we are in the streets he rattles out commands – 'Come here!', 'Don't go there!', 'Hurry up!' These we know to be necessary in our case (because each of us is liable to go wandering off by himself, escaping from Mr Lin and Miss Li). So we docilely breakfast every morning at exactly ten minutes after the time that on the previous evening he has told us we must get up, and are always punctual in getting down to the hotel lobby where he and Miss Li disentangle us from the other tourists, and lead us to our private minibus.

22 May

On our first morning in the capital, we were taken to meet a group of young artists from the Central Academy of Fine Arts. On our way there in the minibus, once we got off the immensely wide Avenue of Perpetual Peace, I was impressed by the Chinese passion for walls. Most of the streets had walls either side, shutting out views of older parts of the town. We passed shop-fronts only a storey high forming screens like stage scenery, beyond the pavement. And behind those flimsy shop-fronts the outlines of higher houses seemed like painted back cloths.

We met the artists – teaching staff and students – not in the Academy itself, but in a reception room off the entrance to an exhibition hall called the National Gallery. The main exhibition there at that moment was of American books, we were told. The reception room into which we were shown was bare and oddly untidy, like a common room for students. On each side there were chairs drawn up against the wall. 'Very Chinese,' said David later, 'their arrangement of furniture, everything pushed up against the wall as though it were a ballroom.' There was a table with a large apple-green thermos flask on it. On one side of a room four young artists were ranged in a row; opposite them David, Gregory and I. At the end of the room, near our two guides, was seated Professor Shao Ta-cheng, editor of a magazine called 'World Fine Arts'. Our hosts, Mr Lin told us, were the Chinese Artists' Association whose headquarters are in this gallery. Only two of the younger Chinese – their names were Mr Tang Mu-li and Mrs Liu Hong – took part in the discussion. The other two, who seemed Tibetan in appearance, whispered to each other, laughing, and pointing at us occasionally like the mysterious Assistants in Kafka's *The Castle*.

Tang Mu-li (a young teacher in his early thirties) had reasons for getting to know David, because, as he told us, he had been offered a place at the Royal College of Art in London. He was worried as to whether he ever would actually get there because fees for foreign students had recently been raised drastically in England. (In fact he did come in September 1981.) Tang Mu-li is bright, friendly, eager, amused. Mrs Liu, a post-graduate student, had a glowing, Madonna-like expression.

The meeting began with tea-sipping and the rather formal introducing of the institution by the senior representative present, a helpful procedure we were to grow very accustomed to in China. 'At this art school,' Professor Shao began, 'they teach painting, sculpture, wood engraving, etching, traditional watercolour painting and art history.' David asked: 'Do you teach landscape painting?' Tang Mu-li answered with bright seriousness: 'Landscape painting is not the major subject taught here, though some students sometimes paint a lot of landscapes.'

I inquired about the position of artists in China. He replied: 'Directly or indirectly the state employs all professional artists.' Tang Mu-li continued: the emphasis of what he said lay on the word 'professional'. We grasped that the distinction between professional and amateur status was institutional in China. If you are classified as an 'amateur' artist you can paint only part of the time. You can, it is true, be admitted to the Artists' Association if your work has merit, but your art has to be secondary to your primary job as a state employee – everyone of course being that. An amateur is, from the point of view of the state, Tang Mu-li said drily, a kind of certified half or quarter artist. 'A professional artist', he said, 'is paid a salary by the state for being an artist, a status assigned by a government department. Sales of art privately between Chinese are not allowed officially.' (We were to see later that artists could pop up suddenly in front of us at beauty spots to sell their wares – but I suppose such sellers correspond merely to those artists in London who flog lightning portrait-sketches they do of people outside the National Portrait Gallery. They fall into no category.)

We were told that the government sometimes commissions works of art. The artist is not paid for the particular painting commissioned other than in the form of the salary he receives as a recognized professional. However, if the work is for export or publication sometimes he does receive a bonus payment for it. The government collects pictures for art galleries and for exhibitions abroad at which it may offer some for sale, and to be shown in tourist hotels (we saw examples of these, to us, depressing official works on display in various hotel foyers).

I asked whether Chinese painters ever sold their works to each other. Tang Mu-li replied: 'Generally Chinese artists don't like to associate their work with the idea of monetary gain. They would consider financial dealings with their colleagues as being harmful to friendship. But sometimes they give each other paintings as gifts.'

There seemed a slight edge to his voice when he added that once the Academy had recognized the existence of an artist he received a salary regardless of what work he produced. And later, a still sharper edge when he said the government sends thousands of students in the sciences abroad annually on scholarships, but only a handful of art students – five, I think he said.

David asked rather pointedly: 'Do you notice that certain artists are very good at painting – better than others? That they have a natural talent and skill which other artists don't have?'

Tang Mu-li took this up seriously: 'That's true in any place. It's impossible to prevent it happening in any country. Some students are very talented. They paint very well but for some reason they can't get recognition. I think there are some in China now . . . It is difficult to judge a painting. That is because of the different points of view of the beholders. For instance, some professors at the college may not like a particular painting, others may like it very much.'

He spoke our, to him foreign, language with precision, a kind of eagerness, as though pleasurably reaching forward for each next word he would say. And smiling.

David asked how a young artist set about attaining recognition as a professional, as distinct from an amateur.

'In general, if you want to be recognized as a professional you have to complete your higher education at college, and then, if the Academy assigns you that position, you get it . . . It's not easy . . . It can happen that a gifted artist finds himself in a position where he is already assigned another job – in engineering, for instance – and the director who is in charge of him as an engineer thinks he should not leave that job – so they don't allow him to become a professional painter – and he has to remain an amateur. Generally, only through continuing his education at college can a student hope to acquire the status of professional painter. However, some amateur artists do get transferred to professional status because they have successfully persuaded the head of the department in which they are employed. But not many.'

While he was saying this I remembered how during the Second World War when I was a fireman, and there was a Ministry of Employment which decided everyone's position, a branch of the Foreign Office wished me to be transferred to Intelligence, and how it took three years to achieve this change of my status. Tang Mu-li's information made us feel a bit glum. He then asked David: 'Are you a professional painter?'

Young artists of the Central Academy

'Yes, yes, I make my living by selling my pictures, but I also work on many other things.' He mentioned the theatre, the opera sets. He remarked that he was now doing designs for Stravinsky's opera *Le Rossignol*, which was based on a story by Hans Christian Andersen on a Chinese theme, with the Japanese as the villains.

The girl, Mrs Liu, echoed: 'A Chinese theme? About the Chinese?'

I asked: 'What do you think of Japanese art here, of Chinese interest in Japanese art?'

Tang Mu-li replied: 'Our Chinese art is . . . The Chinese don't really like modern Japanese art. It's really a combination of Chinese art and Western art. The Chinese don't really like the imitation of Chinese art.'

'Well, I quite see that.'

There was a pause. Then Professor Shao, who evidently had his own previously prepared questions to put to David, asked:

'In your pictures we see elements of Pop and Surrealism. I would like to know: what theories do you hold about Pop Art, Surrealism, abstract art. What do you think of abstract art?'

David answered: 'A lot of it is a bit too remote if all it's about is the artist actually doing it. If that's what it is, then it seems to me a little bit remote from people. But it can also be seen to be like calligraphy; then it can be very beautiful – a brush stroke or a line can be very beautiful. Now we are going back towards realism. I think the problem in the end is that abstraction can be just ornament. There's nothing wrong with ornament; but it's not quite as profound as they claimed, as they led us to believe, really.'

Tang Mu-li inquired how David would characterize his own art. 'I do not give my own work a name. It's for other people to provide labels. That's the job of critics and art historians. It's usually the theoretician who categorizes art. Artists just do their work, don't they, without worrying whether they belong to a particular school.' David asked them what they thought of American art. Tang Mu-li said they felt differently about it according to their individual standpoint. He added vaguely that he thought American painting went in a great many directions. Then he brought the subject back to his own painting. 'As for me, I'm doing research into the theory of realistic art, and so are most Chinese painters, though a few of them work on abstract art. Although we appreciate new techniques and new methods, we like representation, work we can understand. But also we like some abstract paintings, we think them very beautiful. But many Chinese artists have no chance anyway of showing in public abstract art made at home that is beyond the comprehension of most ordinary Chinese people, officials, and exhibition committees.'

Tang Mu-li asked David whether he liked abstract art. David repeated that he was not a theoretician but an artist. 'However,' he went on, 'the problem is, I think, that sometimes people have an urge for novelty, because they wish things to change: and often they start off with a great deal of energy, but after a while the energy evaporates. When the energy is gone, you're left with very little, but when it's there the work does have some spirit. Sometimes I think artists can be more imaginative within limits that are imposed on them. If you are told to make a picture with six lines then you have to be more inventive than if you were told you can employ a hundred lines. . . . But then everything depends on how imaginative the artist really is. I tend to think everything is in the imagination. Abstract art has lost the momentum it had some years ago, certainly.'

Next, Tang Mu-li asked what national exhibitions there were in England. Puzzled, David responded with an 'Er . . .'. Then he hazarded: 'Well, the best is the Royal Academy. It's mostly for amateurs.' Another 'er . . .'.

To break the awkwardness I suggested that the artists show us some of their work. There followed an interval during which they went over to the Central Academy to fetch some. We waited, listening to the banging and shouting going on in the hall outside, a tremendous din. There seemed to be a table at which visitors were signing their names. Finally Tang Mu-li and Mrs Liu returned, laden down with portfolios and some rolled-up canvases. Tang Mu-li showed us academic drawings of nudes, male and female, wearing loin-cloths. He told us that there was much emphasis at this art school on drawing from life. The drawings, David said to us that evening at dinner at the hotel, made him think of student work of some art school in perhaps Rome in 1890. Mrs Liu did large cartoons and drawings on (rather unexpectedly) religious themes illustrating the life of Buddha. These surely, I thought, would not have been permitted during the Cultural Revolution.

A painting Tang Mu-li had done, which was commissioned by the government, was of Mao Tse-tung on horseback surrounded by his followers during some famous episode during the Second World War, he said. The painting was in the heroic style of Soviet socialist realism. In its way, it was very accomplished, as was also a painting, a photograph of which he showed us, of the swooning heroine of some legend in Chinese opera done in the greatest detail. I was overcome by the paradox of socialist revolutions which seem to produce out of their salvationist ideology nothing in art which is not the result of some concept of realism stolen from the stuffiest, most bourgeois academies with, grafted onto this, an overtly revolutionary subject-matter. David scrutinized these paintings very carefully, his face close to them, his eyes screwed up. At last he said: 'Surely this is literalness where everything is put in. But surely with old Chinese painting it wasn't like that.' Tang Mu-li seemed puzzled. He asked: 'Do you mean Chinese traditional painting in watercolour?' 'The Chinese paintings I have seen in watercolour or ink,' David began. Tang Mu-li said: 'Chinese traditional works in watercolour were painted not directly from life, but from memory, and they depict subjects such as emperors in palaces surrounded by courtiers and beautiful courtesans in gardens amid temples and pagodas in a decorative an— exaggerated way. But in oils one can render historic events with accuracy.' He emphasized that his painting of Mao and his cavalry was a historic scene commissioned by the government. After this the students showed us various magazines they had, with reproductions from Picasso, Matisse, etc. They also had the illustrated catalogue of the Tate Gallery.

The Summer Palace

After our morning with the artists, we drove the six miles to the Summer Palace, for luncheon. We entered this great park surrounding Lake Kun Ming by the Eastern Gate and followed the stream of people down a path, uneven and varying in width, sometimes spreading out into other paths, and with little islands of rocks or carvings interrupting the human flow, past the imperial boathouses. On the lake there seemed to be as many people, crowded into boats and rowing, as there were people walking, or standing still, or taking photographs and being photographed, on the shore.

In Peking we had seen hundreds of Chinese on bicycles, or in buses, or marketing, all intent on their purposes, as were the tourists who crowded in the lobbies and dining rooms of the hotel. The Summer Palace was the first place where we saw the Chinese relaxed and enjoying themselves. Here, I thought, the workers have come into their inheritance. They have an air of quiet possession, of taking for granted that they now occupy the palaces of former emperors, targets for seizure or destruction by former European and American powers. Nothing else we saw in China dispelled this overwhelming impression we had of the people enjoying themselves in the grounds and on the water of the Summer Palace.

Later David said that in comparison with the eighteenth-century elegance of the West Lake at Hangchow, the Summer Palace seemed to him very nineteenth century. There was a certain coarseness about it. Perhaps it is this nineteenth-century touch of vulgarity which makes people feel at home here. It is the Hyde Park of Peking.

It is of the nineteenth century for the very good reason that it was rebuilt then by the Empress Dowager Tzu-hsi on the ruins of palaces and other buildings, mostly eighteenth century, which had been pillaged and destroyed by the English and French in 1860. This operation was part of their attempt to dislodge the Manchu Dynasty, already badly shaken by the Taiping revolt, led by the visionary Hong Hsiu Chu'uan, who aspired to establish the kingdom of heaven on earth. The French and British, in common with the Russians, Germans, Greeks and Americans, merely wished to establish the rule of capitalism in China.

The Empress Dowager decided to rebuild the Summer Palace as a place of retirement after her token 'abdication' (while she retained behind-the-scenes power) in favour of her nephew the Emperor Kuang-hsu, when he was nineteen years old. In 1888 she issued a decree stating: 'We conceived the idea of restoring the Ch'in I Yuan [Garden of Clear Rippling Waters], conferring upon it the new name of I Ho Yuan [Garden for the Cultivation of Harmonious Old Age].' To pay for this tremendous undertaking (for which she stated that she had used no public money) she misappropriated funds allocated to modernizing the Chinese navy. The Marble Boat – modelled after a Mississippi paddle boat and berthed – if that is the term – immovably by the lakeside, provides ironic commentary on her patriotism. Its symbolism was not at all lost on Miss Li, who showed it to us with appropriate

indignation. It is a delightful folly, with a saloon and part of the upper deck enclosed by arched columns, and poop culminating in an upcurving stone scroll. It looked to me less like a Mississippi steamer than some little chapel dedicated to a saint in a Gothic cathedral. We went inside to the saloon with its screen of mirrors – somewhat like those in a bar of a Paris brasserie. Miss Li continued to look severe – something of which, with her pleasantly prim features, she was scarcely capable – telling still worse stories of the Empress Dowager. There was a copper steam-boat – originally given to her by the Japanese and recently fished out of the lake – in which she used to go 'cruising' on the lake with her guests.

David and I could not help feeling a little sympathy for the Empress Dowager, thinking how splendid it would be if Mr Brezhnev or President Reagan allocated the vast sums appropriated by their governments for nuclear armaments to building, well, a marble spaceship.

We walked back along the lake shore till we came to the painted corridor, and had luncheon at the Ting Li Guan restaurant, in a building which used to be a theatre. Afterwards, we walked along the covered corridor, looking at the pictures of famous landscapes and legends painted on its beams. Halfway along it, David and Gregory left me to climb up the many steps of the Hill of Longevity to the Bronze Kiosk. There they got a view of the roofs of palaces far beneath them, a complex of interlocking rectangles.

Mr Lin and Miss Li accompanied David and Gregory. Alone, I started looking for somewhere to sit down (always a major undertaking in China) and enjoy the pleasant atmosphere of May at the Summer Palace. People were ingenious at finding places to rest. Some youths had stretched themselves on the top of the balustrades along the corridor, leaning back against the supporting columns.

People walked about looking contented, side by side, but no couples held hands, or if a boy and girl did, one knew they must be Overseas Chinese. I thought an analogous scene in the West would have had to be a village green, perhaps in New England, in the early nineteenth century. The Chinese whom I saw walking here did not look sexually repressed, but they did perhaps look puritanical. They certainly were discreet.

The others returned. Miss Li took us further along the covered corridor to the theatre in the Palace of Virtue and Harmony which provided the Empress Dowager with her favourite entertainment. It has a throne and chairs where the Empress sat with her followers watching the stage, on a platform which seems almost a stage itself; as though she provided a spectacle as much to be looked at as the actors. She herself chose the plays that were performed, from the mostly Buddhist classical repertoires she knew well. Sometimes she chose to appear among the all-male cast of a play, usually in the role of the goddess of Mercy (Kuan Yin).

We were shown the Jade Waves Palace where, for ten years, the Emperor Kuang-hsu was imprisoned, after the debacle of the conspiracy which he frenetically encouraged in 1898 to liberate himself and China from the reactionary Empress Dowager and to become the head of a government of reform and modernization. He had envisaged a rule of scholars and mystics putting into effect the ideas of the prolific writer, reformist, modernizer, idealist K'ang Yu-wei.

Miss Li showed us this and other places which provided evidence of the Empress Dowager's wickedness. David's and my eyes met. We were, both at the same moment, struck by the thought that she was using almost the same words to describe the Empress Dowager as we had heard used to describe Chiang Ch'ing, the wife of Mao – who also had a passion for the theatre.

One wonders whether the Chinese enjoying themselves in the Summer Palace felt the same indignation about the Empress Dowager as we were supposed to imbibe from Miss Li. Perhaps they did not feel the presence of this Sitwellian ghost. To us, however, there was something about the atmosphere of the Summer Palace that made it feel like many Victorian parks and gardens: that it was presided over by some fairy godmother, perhaps wicked but with a magic wand just the same.

The Summer Palace is certainly impressive, but it is not awesome and over-whelming, in the manner of the Forbidden City; nor does it convey a sense of the sacred, as do Buddhist temples and the Temple of Heaven.

Since returning home I have read Marina Warner's *The Dragon Empress*, a book which despite its monstrous subject-matter – the concubine Tzu-Hsi who became the Empress Dowager, in all but name the ruler of China – has cast the spell of hindsight over my memories of the Summer Palace. I feel the presence of the

Steps leading to the Bronze Kiosk

Empress Dowager brooding over these palaces, gardens and temples, especially over the Palace of Joy and Longevity where she took up residence for eight months of each year during the period of her nominal retirement, between 1889 and 1898. Every week her nephew, the Emperor Kuang-hsu – frustrated, isolated and easily excitable, collector of clocks and convert to the idea of vast reforms modernizing the Chinese Empire – left the Forbidden City where he was in name ruler and came to pay her a 'filial' visit at the Summer Palace in order to receive 'instructions' from her. I see her concealed behind the screen Miss Li showed us, whispering to her nephew seated on his throne the answers he should give to visiting dignitaries.

The Empress Dowager is as haunting a presence in the Summer Palace as Queen Victoria at Balmoral. Carried by bearers from place to place in the grounds of the Summer Palace, with its lake, its landscape transformed to remind her of places she loved in the neighbourhood of Hangchow where she spent her youth, she would suddenly command her retinue to stop and take a picnic at some view-point which struck her fancy. The picnic is spread out with its hundred dishes, eighty of them putrescent because her servants know that although she orders a hundred to be served each day, there are only twenty that she fancies. I think of her suddenly disgracing one of her followers, in front of all the others, and having him beaten with bamboo rods that a servant always carries in expectation of such an emergency; and of her doing watercolours and calligraphy, and having a portrait of Queen Victoria, with whom she identified, by her bedside, and following that monarch's career with envious fascination, and rejoicing when Victoria died and she outlived her rival.

Tyrannical, narrow-minded, voracious, and downright murderous, nevertheless she was a woman of taste and affections with something about her behaviour and appearance – Lewis Carrollish – which does provide a grotesque caricature of Victoria: as, surely, there is something about the Empress of India, ruler of the British Empire, a faint whiff of the Empress Dowager. One can just imagine that after the death of Albert, had she been unprincipled and in a position of power equal with that of the Dragon Empress, Victoria might have appropriated vast sums of money from the British navy for building not just one Memorial to Albert but hundreds of them all over England. And does not the image of the Empress Dowager whispering to Kuang-hsu the answers he should give bring to mind a Max Beerbohm cartoon of Queen Victoria seated at the centre of an enormous purple carpet, sending her eldest son, the Prince of Wales, the future Edward VII, into the corner of the room?

In the evening we had drinks at the British Embassy, on the terrace of the Residence, which resembled a large and comfortable English country house in that part of Peking which is now a reserve for foreign diplomats. Besides Sir Percy Cradock, the Ambassador, there were Mr Hunter, whom we had met yesterday, and the commercial attaché. From the terrace we looked out over a beautiful garden. Later on we met other diplomats and visitors on special missions, some of them at the

Summer Palace, architectural details

hotel. I formed some impressions which were really of views of officials in the West about present-day China.

A journalist expressed the opinion that, after all the Chinese had been through during the past fifteen years, their country was now going through a 'period of retrenchment and rightism'. The result of this change was that the left had been put down and would not come back.

Remembering the left of the English Labour Party, I said I thought it unusual for leftists to accept defeat except for a limited period and for tactical reasons. Moreover, in the past, political leaders in China had frequently had set-backs, and later been rehabilitated. Might not the Gang of Four stage a come-back? The journalist said that two of them were under a suspended death sentence, which meant that even if, when their case was reviewed, they were not executed, they would remain in prison for life. The other two were too old to have any future anyway. I said, 'All the same, what would happen if, in some form or other, the left did come back?' He answered by saying that they had made such a mess of things that if they ever did so, China would be finished – finished for a hundred years. He said that, as a result of the Cultural Revolution, China was already greatly weakened in several respects. A whole generation of the young had missed out on their education. If we were taken to any factories, we would notice the great weakness of the Chinese in management, the result of the persecution of this class of person during the Cultural Revolution.

Some further remarks I noted down were: China is not one of the super-powers on account of its armaments, in which it is at least thirty years behind America and Russia, but because it covers a quarter of the globe and has a population of approximately a thousand million. A militarily weak China can, nevertheless, in alliance with America, tie up x number of Russian divisions on the frontier between the two countries.

Writers and artists are organized within their official associations. Everyone who gets published is an officially approved writer. Writers and artists are aware of what is permitted and what is not permitted. There was a time, two years ago (the winter of 1978–79), when some very open and critical statements were put up as posters on Democracy Wall in Peking. Then there was a crackdown and now there are no more such declarations and debates.

All such remarks seemed received impressions about China, but even now, afterwards, when I have read several books, it seems difficult to get beyond received ideas. Underlying all that I read and heard said, there seems to be an assumption that, though everything is undetermined, the end of an era has been reached and that the present stage of pragmatic government is somehow a conclusion. After many errors of practice and theory, all the lessons have been learned. From now on the rulers of China are going to govern by reason. Instead of ideological Marxist 'recognition of necessity' in order to achieve communism, there will be general agreement to do whatever is necessary to run the government and the economy on a day to day basis.

It is like an epilogue: post-Maoism is a post mortem on the mistakes Mao made – the Hundred Flowers, the Great Leap Forward, the Cultural Revolution. Fortunately, what he said can be separated from these acts. Quotations from Mao's thoughts and sayings provide endless calligraphy on walls, signing whatever actions future governments undertake, like a blank cheque.

Belief in the reasonableness of the utterances of the generations of leaders now in power relies partly on the fact that they themselves, in their own lives, their own antiquated flesh, embody the sum of the experiences of the revolution, from the Long March onwards, and thus speak out of the learned and experienced wisdom of that generation. At the same time, this, if conclusive, is also an end, with time running out in those very minds and bodies, their inevitable physical decay. But what they had is exactly what the young lack – the adventure of the Long March or any such beginning, as David pointed out during our conversations. So one has the curious impression that this conclusion of pragmatism and reason is also an end. It means little or nothing to the younger generation who lack the myth and the adventure.

23 May

Mr Lin had arranged for us to visit the office of 'Poetry Magazine' on the outskirts of the city. It was in a row of shed-like one-storey buildings which had the look of having been put up in a hurry with a view to tearing them down soon. Just as with the artists, our hosts seemed to wish us to understand that these were only temporary quarters which they were occupying. The room in which we met was smaller than that at the National Gallery, but similar in its general appearance: bare walls, a table, chairs against the walls. On the table, cups, and a large fluorescent-green thermos flask.

The three poets sat in a row against the wall on one side of the room, David, Gregory and I sat opposite them. David placed a sketchbook on the table and started a sketch of the green thermos with, beyond it, two of the poets.

Our senior host was Mr Tsou Di-fan, Deputy Chairman of 'Poetry Magazine', and himself a poet. He was middle-aged, keen-eyed, intent, with a bird-like face. The other poets to whom Mr Tsou introduced us were Miss Li Hsiao-yu, who looked like a heroine of labour in a movie about a fishing village – broad-faced with twists of black hair falling down each side of her face over her ears – and Ch'iu Hsiao-lung, a tall young man, wearing horn-rimmed spectacles, who had an earnest expression.

The meeting followed the formula with which we were beginning to become familiar. We sat down, hosts on one side of the table, guests on the other, with our guides, who partly acted as interpreters, at the end of the room. Cups were filled with tea, and Mr Tsou, as the senior officer of the magazine present, told us about it.

'Poetry Magazine', he explained, had a readership of 100,000. The poems published are largely on themes of Construction, Modernization, Nature and Love.

The young poets: Ch'iu Hsiao-lung and Miss Li Hsiao-yu

The poets

(Here there followed something about the Four Modernizations, I think.) Recently, 'Poetry Magazine' had broadened its interests but circulation had fallen. The motto of the magazine was 'Let the hundred flowers blossom', chosen because today so many magazines are permitted to be published. It struck me that, considering the fate that befell so many of Mao's hundred flowers, this seemed an ironic motto to choose. But I note a tendency to acquit Chairman Mao of responsibility for the consequences of his edicts.

Like Tang Mu-li, the artist, Mr Tsou dwelt on the difference between professional and amateur: the professional being by definition one whom the state permits to work full time at his art. He said that most poets over sixty received salaries.

Recently the quality of poetry has been raised, he said, a bit as though he were speaking of livestock. The reason for the improvement was that poets are now permitted to cover a far wider range of subjects than some years previously. There was an opening up now of themes of nature, countryside, rivers, landscapes, also love and friendship. During the period of the Gang of Four these had been taboo, particularly love. The idea then was that all poets should expatiate on the virtues of that heroine, Chairman Mao's wife. Criticism of the errors of the establishment was not allowed. For example, the government declared a village called Tachai (Dahzai) in Shensi (Shaanxi) province to be a wonderful example of the success of the rural production brigades. It became a place of pilgrimage for tours (until it became something of a laughing stock). Writers were expected to write saying how successful it was, though it was a failure. 'People had to say false words . . . After smashing up the Gang of Four, we had the opportunity to study the criterion of truth. . . . Now poets can write according to their wish.'

I tried to discover what was meant by the criterion of truth. The young poet, Ch'iu Hsiao-lung, explained that they could put a broad interpretation on their commitment to write poetry about people who were engaged in constructive tasks. 'For instance,' he said, 'if we today write poems about love and beauty and natural scenery, we think these can be good poems. Moreover, such poems can really educate people and enhance their ideological role.'

During the Gang of Four period, poems were labelled bad if they did not conform to directives by officials who were not poets. But today the criticism of poetry was the preserve of the poets themselves. Poets were encouraged to go in for self-criticism in the course of discussion.

I asked what were their aims in writing poetry. The first to answer was Miss Li Hsiao-yu. She was rather bashful. She explained that she had gone to the Victory Oil Field in eastern China. There she worked together with the oil workers, and wrote poems about their lives. She had published a volume called *Ode to the Feather of White Geese*. 'A charming title,' I said. 'She also writes love poems,' interposed Mr Tsou, to put her in the best possible light, I suppose.

She went on: 'I hadn't been writing long before I approached "Poetry Magazine". At that time I was in the army, and there I had the opportunity to live and work with the soldiers. I tried to write poems about army life. After making contact with "Poetry Magazine" I had the opportunity to go to different places, one of which was the oilfield. Then I thought I should write something about their life, their struggle.' She did not insist that the only kind of poetry that should be written was the socialist realist kind.

She said that young poets had different approaches to writing poetry. Some wished to express their own personal feelings and ideas, their way of thinking. She, however, constructed her poems on the foundations laid by writers during the 1950s and 1960s, who were trying to write about real conditions.

'Then what is your attitude towards the expression of your feelings in your poetry?' She answered, 'I feel satisfied with my poetry when it expresses happiness and pleasure in the workers' lives. I really do feel that my thinking is in accord with their thinking, and so I am very happy with that.'

Her dark eyes shone. She said all this modestly, demurely even, not as though she considered herself an example for others to follow.

David asked, 'Do the oil workers read your poems and find that they express their attitudes?' 'The workers read my poems,' she answered, 'not only the workers in the oilfield where I worked, but also other workers from other oilfields. They write me letters expressing satisfaction with my poems. Moreover, members of the Ministry of the Petroleum Industry said my poems were good.'

I asked our local guide to translate one of her poems for me. Miss Li did so, rather approximately, as was inevitable. Later Mr Lin produced a more studied version (which I have slightly amended). The poem is called 'Moon in the Meridian Transit' and runs – in what I suppose gives only a rough idea of it – as follows:

> *Wind from the rigs brings over the smell of the oil.*
> *The horizon is twinkling in the deep night,*
> *The hum of the machinery praises these most memorable days*
> *O, this moonbeam . . .*
> *Tonight what shall I talk with you about,*
> *And how . . .*

Next, I asked the scholarly looking young man to talk about his work. He explained modestly: 'As a matter of fact, I'm not really a poet, only a student of poetry who tries to do some translations. I'm interested in English and American poetry, especially Eliot's and some of Auden's, particularly his poem written in China about the Chinese people's war against the Japanese. I try my best to translate good poems with good technique.'

'Have you ever read any American poetry?'

'Allen Ginsberg's "Howl".' He added that he liked my poem 'Landscape Near an Aerodrome'.

'What do you look for in a poem?'

'I think I look for technique which I find in Eliot's poems and also in the English Metaphysical poets, especially John Donne.'

He added that the Chinese Classical poetry which he and certain other poets of his generation mostly admired was that of the T'ang Dynasty (AD 618–907). On the plane David and I had been reading a Penguin selection of works of this period, so we saw the point of his liking this esoteric writing. He added that he was also interested in writing prose poems.

When Ch'iu Hsiao-lung rendered his poem 'Today' for us in approximative English (with help from our interpreter and from Mr Lin) I understood better his interest in metaphysical poetry, however rudimentary the translation. Again I am grateful to Mr Lin for transcribing an improved (though, he said, very imperfect) version of this:

> *Not merely because an icy yesterday is still fresh in the mind*
> *Not merely because tomorrow with buds is waiting*
> *Do I love thee, O Today, so warmly,*
> *But because where would life be if there were not today.*
> *If I did not love thee, but lingered in yesterday's disillusionment,*
> *Life would be one sigh – as in a dream.*
> *If I did not love thee today, but sat idly waiting for tomorrow to emerge,*
> *Life would only be a yawn – as if preceding a dream.*

Again, a suggestion of the Gang of Four and the suffering caused during the Cultural Revolution, it seemed to me. That, surely, is the 'yesterday' referred to in the poem. Today is an era of comparative freedom, a budding. At the same time, the mood of the poet reflects a certain uneasiness about tomorrow, as he well may feel, I thought.

Miss Li attempted next to translate a poem by Mr Tsou. The poem was difficult and it was no fault of hers if she stumbled, helped out a bit though she was by Mr Lin. The poem was called 'Shore'. 'In it', said Mr Lin, 'the poet expresses his hatred for the endless political agitation during the period of the Gang of Four. He yearns for stability and peace, using the sea as a metaphor for his state of mind.' Miss Li translated:

> *After a long time sail on the sea . . .*
> *I have been on the sea too long . . . yet one small piece*
> *of it, like a patch of grass, is still . . .*
> *It is not floating tranquil and stable . . . that is destiny . . .*

Her voice trailed off: 'Oh, it is almost impossible . . .'

I asked: 'What happened to poets during the Cultural Revolution?' Mr Tsou said: 'In some cases they were sent to the countryside, to the cadre schools where they had to do hard physical labour. Those who were lucky enough to stay in town had to do menial jobs like cleaning offices. Some just could not stand the great political pressure brought on them. They committed suicide. Some were sent to prison. Take myself for example. I was sent to the cadre school and made to work in the vegetable garden.'

'He is one of our best poets,' said Mr Lin. 'One of his poems was published in the *People's Daily*. The title is 'If There Were Not Flowers'. He took up a volume and began:

If there were not flowers in this world, how could there be sweet or sour fruit? How could the bees arrive, and how could the children know how sweet life is, if there were not flowers in this world?
When the boys and girls, deep in love, are singing, is it likely that they will always give one another the classical masterpieces? Or is it not far more likely that they will give each other just some biscuits or honey, . . .

Mr Lin trailed off apologetically, then he bravely started again:

Oh, without the love of the night-blossoming flowers, how lonely the world would be.
If there were no flowers in the world, how could we speak of friendship all over the world?

He gave up attempting to translate further. The conversation turned to other matters. Ch'iu Hsiao-lung, the scholarly student, said that for poets there had been little contact between China and the West since the 1930s, and they were anxious to resume contact now. Could I help them make a selection of poets published in English since then, so that they could translate them? He said that Chinese people now wanted very much to open up to the West. Certain works of Freud were being translated. They said all these things very hopefully. At various times, the conversation touched on the subject of poetry and the masses. They appeared to agree that poetry should be written in simple language so that it was easily comprehensible by the masses. They said that one English poet who had visited them had not agreed, and they seemed baffled and a bit hurt by this.

David said that there was, in Western countries, a popular culture of song lyrics – jazz, Rock, the Beatles, etc. – which was widely diffused but which no one would call the poetry of the people. Moreover, if one read these lyrics as poetry they were, for the most part, disappointing. He asked them whether popular songs in Chinese were what they would call the poetry of the people. They shook their heads at this. They seemed to agree that what they wrote was both poetry by their own standards – which were not those of lyrics for popular songs – and also meant for the people, the 'masses'.

I thought that they were probably referring to the poems they had shown us, which certainly had a political meaning as well as a personal one. They think that poetry should, in a very wide sense, be about the situation in which the Chinese find themselves at particular moments in their history. In their view, the poet should be a guide.

Afterwards, I thought that the poets we met were, like the painters, undoubtedly anxious to have a genuine exchange of ideas. They were not cynical. At the same time, they were restrained. There were limits to what they could tell and discuss. The boundaries of how far they could go were defined by the mythology of Chinese politics. According to this, the Gang of Four are seen as villains and what they stood for, such as the complete politicization of literature and the limitations imposed on subject-matter, has now been discredited. But blown-up photographs of Chairman Mao remain buoyant, his calligraphy remains a signature tune for behaviour, and a Chinese wall of what is called Marxist-Leninist-Maoist thought surrounds everything. The poets, like the painters, seemed to walk warily and hint that 'we hope for more freedom' in voices that were unconcealedly tentative.

A metaphor formed in my mind of conversation with these Chinese: that of a clear transparent stream with a smiling friendly surface, but a few inches down an opaque floor of stone at the bottom of the stream below which one could not see at all. Within certain limits, they discuss everything freely, openly, seriously, sincerely, but the limits to their clarity are as clear as the clarity itself.

I can only admire the courage and hope with which the Chinese press against the boundaries of their freedom, after so many advances followed by reverses – the hundred flowers allowed to blossom, only to be withered by the state.

When one considers the many occasions, beginning even before the Revolution, on which the Chinese Communist Party has allowed writers some degree of freedom, and then used their exercise of that limited freedom as justification for persecuting them, one is amazed at the recurrence of the phrase, 'the hundred flowers', which might seem to have a sinister connotation. Jonathan D. Spence, in his authoritative book *The Gate of Heavenly Peace*, writes that Mao Tse-tung, having sponsored in 1957 the 'new criticism movement' and supported greater freedom of expression which included putting up wall-posters in Peking,

decided to end it, in late June 1957, and inaugurated a new 'anti-rightist' campaign, claiming in his own defense that he had 'let the demons and hobgoblins out of their lairs in order to wipe them out better, and let the seeds sprout in order to make it more convenient to hoe them.'

Letting things out and then pulling them in seems to have been a pattern of behaviour with Mao. The hundred flowers would surely be far better named 'the hundred mice'. Again and again the mice are allowed by the State to play awhile and then when they go too far a large paw stretches out and pulls them back into the cat's jaws. Constant repetition of this process may make one wonder whether the very freedom of the mice to play around a bit, during some period in which they are let out, is not evidence more of their enslavement than of their freedom. They are allowed to play at being free for a few weeks or months or even years, and are then pulled back.

Their freedom is not the freedom of the writer but of the politician to let them out a bit. Where there is a political rationale for every intellectual activity, everything is politics. Worse even than that, the politician is everyone or, rather, the man to whose existence all other existences refer.

Once, looking at a portrait of Mao Tse-tung stuck up on some crimson wall, Rimbaud's phrases 'on me pense' and 'je est un autre', expressing the wish of the

poet to short-circuit that area of consciousness in him which calls himself 'I' and make himself an instrument of the universe outside him, acting directly upon his sensibility as poet, came into my mind. It occurred to me that translated into the language of Maoism, or Marxist-Leninist-Maoist thought, what is required of the Chinese poet is that he should say 'Mao me pense' and 'je est Mao': Mao thinks me and what in me calls itself 'I' has to be thought of as Mao. This is the substitution of political for poetic consciousness, and in fact the submission of all other consciousness to the political. The possibility always exists that only in this way could a country like China achieve social justice for 'the masses'.

Tien An Men Square and the Imperial City

David said that what struck him most about China was contrasts: of town and country, the imperial past and the socialist present, the old and the new, the young and the old. Contrast, indeed, is dramatized at the double centre of the capital, with the juxtaposition of the Forbidden City (or the Imperial City, as it is now called), the centre of power of the ancient Chinese Empire, and Tien An Men Square, centre of the Chinese People's Republic. The two meet at the Tien An Men (Gate of Heavenly Peace), where on very great occasions the Emperor would cause the imperial edicts to be let down to kneeling officials who received them from the mouth of a golden phoenix; and where now the portrait of Mao Tse-tung is hung, his face superimposed on six hundred years of history, looking like a postage stamp affixed to a huge crimson envelope addressed to the future. It is flanked by the slogans in giant's calligraphy: 'Long Live the People's Republic of China' and 'Long Live the Great Union Between the Peoples of the World'.

I suggested to David that he should do a schematic drawing contrasting the Imperial Palace and Tien An Men Square. Later on he did this.

There is at some points a fusion of contrasting opposites. Each acquires the characteristics of the other, a reversal of roles. Imperialism and modern socialism seem two sides of the same coin, national or nationalist. The Imperial Palace and the socialist Tien An Men Square have one overriding factor in common: a megalomaniac vastness.

Tien An Men Square was extended, with much destruction of old buildings and walls, to its present size in 1958, enabling an area which had long been the scene of demonstrations against the imperial rulers and foreigners to become larger than the Forbidden City, thus fulfilling its historic role. Today, the area of this vast square, the greatest in the world, exceeds that of the Imperial Palace. The train of the future has overtaken that of the past, for all the world to see. The Chinese, who are extremely aware of the capacity of numinous places to become poetic symbols in history, will not forget this.

In their very vastness, the two have also in common a certain air of perpetually waiting. The Forbidden City – the Imperial City – might today be called the Forbidding City: it is so overwhelming in emptiness, so chilling to the visitor, belonging so utterly to its vanished past which filled it with life. The tourists in its great courtyards, halls and temples, seem as alien and separate from it as does the sea that washes at the feet of a granite cliff. We the tourists were, I thought, a mockery among these completely emptied buildings. The Imperial City awaits past Chinas. In its contrasting way, Tien An Men Square also has the air of waiting: not for the dead but for the living – perhaps for the unborn – the masses.

Having read about the demonstrations in homage to Mao Tse-tung which took place here during the Cultural Revolution – apocalyptic almost – and the almost miraculous events of 5 April 1976, following the death of Premier Chou En-lai, on the occasion of his funeral – when tens of thousands of Chinese protested against the removal by the authorities of wreaths heaped up in his memory on the Heroes' Monument – the image, in my mind, of the masses ceases simply to be that of the million or so who fill Tien An Men Square on May Day and for official parades. It becomes something much more like an embodied will of the people choosing in times of division between leaders and policies. In China, on occasion, 'the masses' represent – in practical terms – a force that has a momentum of its own which creates the future.

The Imperial City is haunted by the past and the dead, Tien An Men Square is haunted by the future and the living. For the Forbidden City the Imperial China has passed away for ever; for Tien An Men Square communism has not yet, in its final form, appeared.

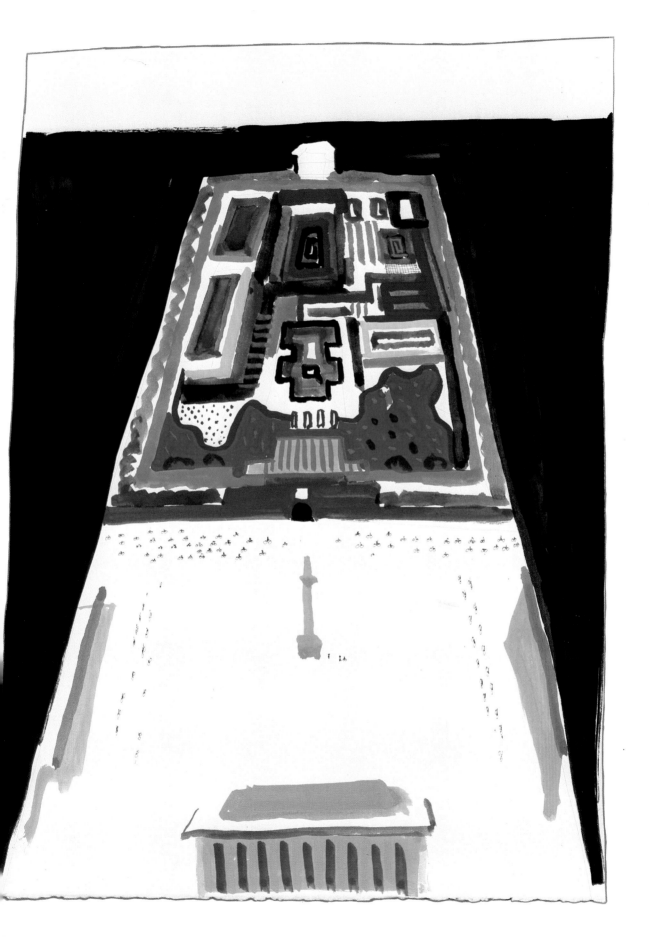

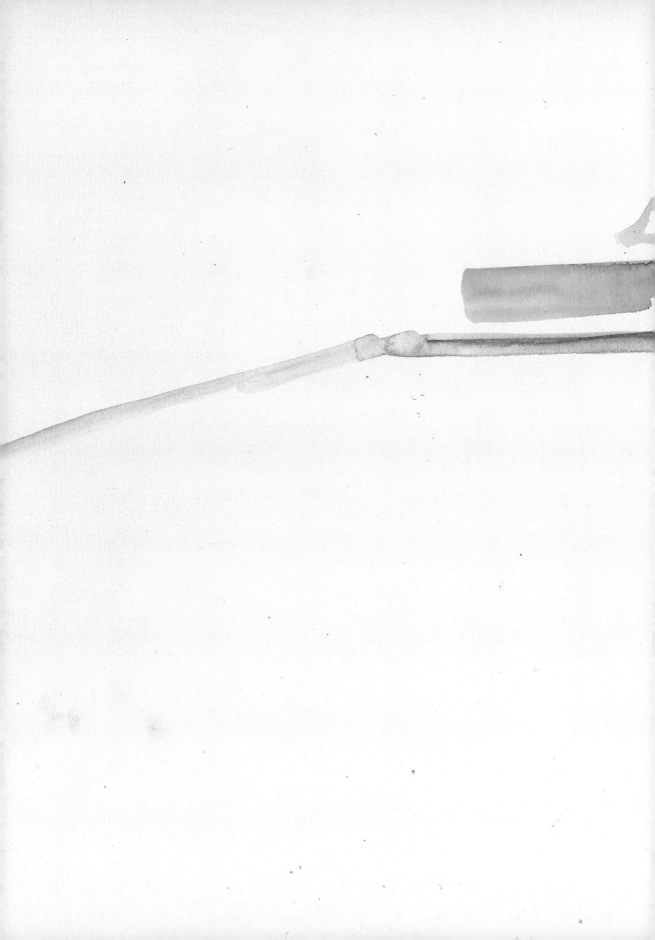

The architecture of both areas provides the guides with occasion for enumerating those reams of statistics which seem, in their mouths, a manifestation of the millions of the Chinese in all places and at all times, above and under the soil. The Imperial Palace, we were told, was built between 1407 and 1420, employing over that period of time 200,000 workers. The Mao Tse-tung Memorial Hall was built between October 1976 and August 1977 by 700,000 volunteers.

A guidebook which I buy at the Imperial Palace tells me that the miracles of art and architecture there are proof of the genius of the Chinese people. True, of course, but the argument backfires when one looks at the architecture of Tien An Men Square, if it is considered the expression – even more assertively, and a bit dubiously – of the genius of Chinese workers. The buildings of the imperialist past and the socialist present could not be clearer examples of the contrast that David noticed everywhere: one seems simply the negation of the other. But, other than vastness, what both have in common is anonymity: the lack of any character that might suggest individual architects and artists. Both are the expression of their age: a choice which is completely linked with the power of the rulers at their particular times in history.

I suppose it might be said that the buildings in Tien An Men Square express the idea of the greatness of the people realized by the dictatorship of the proletariat. If this is the case, it is strange that the buildings have so much in common with totalitarian architecture elsewhere: Stalin's, Mussolini's, Hitler's and, in capitalist societies, great industrial concerns and banks. Gregory remarked that the Mao Tse-tung Memorial Hall reminded him of the Home Federal Savings Bank at Sunset Boulevard and Vine, in Los Angeles.

Overleaf: view from Peking hotel window

Some of the books I have read emphasize the continuity of China. This, I am sure, is true of the countryside, villages, old parts of town, the Peking Opera, the hobbies Chinese delight in, food, the ways in which peasants still work in many places, and the traditionalism we were to note in the calligraphy and drawings done by many artists. But the monuments of past eras seemed for the most part to show the complete breaking off today of a tradition, the utter lack of connection of the revolution with the past. To imagine the burial of an Emperor – his corpse carried down the Sacred Way – at the Eastern Tombs would be as difficult for us as to imagine the burial of a pharaoh in a pyramid. Nor do the Chinese, like the Egyptians, go in for *son et lumière* in which such a funeral might be re-enacted. Perhaps they will one day do this.

The Imperial City seems remote, completely discontinuous from the present represented by Tien An Men Square. The very perfection of the state of preservation, or restoration, in which it is maintained makes it seem the more so: like some marvellous shell, gleaming, polished, pink and brown, mottled on the outside, mother-of-pearl lined within, but with the life inside extinct. The very fact of its no longer being the Forbidden City but the most visited and toured-over of places acts as a kind of exorcism of the ceremony, ritual, sacredness and pomp that emblazoned its past. Perhaps indeed the life was gone already long before the end of the Manchu Dynasty when the Empress Dowager Tzu-hsi first received the wives of Europeans. I do not mean here to bemoan its passing.

An empty shell, and broken off completely from today, yet prodigiously haunted, not only a ghost city, but a city positively teeming, overflowing with ghosts. Hierarchies inconceivable in terms of modern China and us tourists haunt throne-room and courtyard. Every ghost is in his place in accordance with his rank and station in precisely measured ordinances and rituals: the members of the royal family, the courtiers, the priests, the generals, the concubines, the eunuchs. The timetable of the rulers and their attendants is accounted for every month of every year, every day of every month, every hour of every day. But we, unloaded from buses and charabancs, carrying cameras, having things explained to us by guides, are less than ghosts here. We are the hollow men, shadows only.

It seemed to me strange that the Chinese, apart from doing a lot of renovating and re-painting, seem to emphasize the dead distances of everything ancient. They do not attempt to galvanize this corpse of the Imperial City: hoist the great flags and banners and pennons, ring the bells, wind up the clocks so fancied by several emperors. In Venice, in front of St Mark's, on fête days, they run up on masts three enormous flags with, embroidered on them, insignia of the city; the masts seem to rise to the full height of the dome behind them, with the flags, reaching down to the top of the portico, undulating in the sea winds.

But Venice, of course, preserves continuity with its own past which it constantly recreates: there is an archbishop; high mass is celebrated in the Duomo; there are gondolas and gondoliers; even tourism is a tradition going back hundreds of years. There are times in China when the tourists seem totally disconnected from the places they are visiting – even when these are automobile factories – like the plug of the television set in David's and Gregory's room which failed to fit into its socket.

We passed between high crimson walls along a thoroughfare crowded with tourists, and entered – through the Meridian Gate – an immense courtyard paved with quite small stones intensely white under the sky. There we saw five marble-balustraded bridges across the bow-shaped channel of the River of Gold which traverses the courtyard, and whose banks also have marble balustrades. Crossing one of these bridges, we were confronted by a long building with six red-painted columns visible below a long yellow-tiled roof which had slightly upcurving ends and above it, separated only by a narrow cleft of shadow between roofs, another much higher roof with ends much more definitely up-tilted. This, Miss Li informed us, was the Gate of Supreme Harmony – Tai Ho Men. The Gate of Supreme Harmony was flanked symmetrically on either side by four small buildings: the first a roofed wall; the second a little roofed hall with columns; the third a roofed wall; the fourth a small double roofed watch-tower. At this point there was a much longer roofed wall at right-angles to it and partly enclosing this side of the court-yard. All these buildings were painted red and roofed with the same yellow tiles as the Imperial Palace.

The Gate of Supreme Harmony is really a grandiose porch, a reception place for visitors who may rest there and then pass through to the second great courtyard, on the further side of which there is the Hall of Supreme Harmony, Tai Ho Tien. This is a more exalted version of the Gate, and, like it, stands above triple platforms. It also has double roofs paralleled in the same way, but more splendid. Ten red-painted columns are visible in front, as against the six of the Gate which we saw as we approached it.

The effect of triple platforms enclosed in rectangular balustrades, only inter-rupted at those intervals where steps or slabs of ramps lead down from platform to platform (and these also have balustrades), is of exalting the Hall of Supreme Harmony in highly ornamental marble frames that enclose its space, as though upon an altar with altar railings. The great halls of the Imperial Palace are treated as supremely precious objects, elevated on triple steps, and enclosed in their triple marble frames.

Behind the Hall of Supreme Harmony, sharing the same triple platform, are the two other supreme halls. Between the two great ones, the Hall of Supreme Harmony and, slightly smaller, the Hall of the Preservation of Harmony (Pao Ho Tien), is the much smaller Hall of Perfect Harmony (Chung Ho Tien), square, with columns on all sides and a pyramidal concave roof. In relation to the others, the Hall of the Preservation of Harmony looks almost like a pavilion but it holds its place at the centre, like a navel.

The white marble balustrades and the columns framing these halls reminded me of marquees. The thought that came into my mind when I first saw them, sym-metrically arranged along the central axis of the three such north-south axes on which the Imperial City is built – was *The Field of the Cloth of Gold* at Hampton

Court. I thought of the Imperial City not so much as the embellished enlargement of the ground plan of a single traditional Chinese house – with its courtyard and arrangement of outer lesser rooms and screens protecting the greater ones – as the splendid gold-tented encampment of some conquering army where the Emperor's tent is the core and all lesser dwellings are related to it with obeisant military symmetry. The halls, with their upturned roofs which are supported on wooden frames that rest on immensely strong painted wooden columns and are criss-crossed by a complicated system of beams and rafters, also made me think of tent-like forms, just as I associate the structure of a Greek temple with that of a log cabin.

The interiors of these halls are – with their highly ornamented and painted ceilings which are not structural but, like the walls, false, with their screens, their brocades, their furnishings, their bronze and enamel trophies, their incense-burners, their sculptures of animals and mythological beasts – all of a highly movable kind, pieces in a game of endless ritual and ceremony. The Imperial City with streaming pennons, trumpets, clanging bells and gongs was a stage set for the continuous re-enactment of imperial, military and priestly ritual.

We were shown the throne on which the Emperor sat in the Hall of Perfect Harmony, preparatory to sitting on that in the Hall of Supreme Harmony; and preparatory to sitting enthroned in the Hall of the Preservation of Harmony while giving banquets for ambassadors and other dignitaries.

David was, I think, a bit chilled by the overwhelming Imperial Palace in all its vast external show and inner desolation: 'It looks as if the whole place had been

looted and ransacked,' he said after we had been shown the interior of the Hall of Supreme Harmony. He was, of course, right. Looted many times in recent history, it was finally despoiled of its greatest treasures by Chiang Kai-shek when he abandoned Peking and went to Taiwan.

What delighted him were details: rafters barely protruding under vermilion-painted eaves with their circular ends embossed like medallions and painted in a great variety of colours, showing through violet shadows; the tops of banisters chiselled into twisted shapes of torch flames; columns above balustrades looking like the tops of field-marshals' batons; the dragons, creatures of heaven and earth, like fiery wriggling octopi, with heads of snarling heraldic beasts on the great Nine Dragon Screen with its overhanging margins of tiled roofing.

Most of all he admired, here and at the Eastern Tombs, the bas-reliefs such as that on the great stone slab between the steps leading to the Hall of the Preservation of Harmony. In this energetic relief of dragons, scaly and clawed, the clouds, stylized clusters of whorls clinging to each other, have the incredibly precise look of amoebae or bacilli on a slide seen through a microscope. Chiselled in stone, they are handled with the kind of mastery that Leonardo showed in ink and sanguine on paper when he drew whirlpools, storm clouds or human hair. I thought of Yeats' poem 'Sailing to Byzantium':

> *Nor is there singing school but studying*
> *Monuments of its own magnificence.*

24 May

We went to the Eastern Tombs, about three hours' drive from Peking, 74 miles east of the city along the tree-lined dusty road which was dense with every kind of traffic, but hardly any private cars except for the occasional one probably hired by tourists. There were buses, vans, lorries, tractors, horse-drawn carts, sometimes carts drawn by two donkeys, carts pushed by human beings, bicycles, bicycles, bicycles. This very slow traffic tended to move at the average speed of the whole – the slowest being the cart-pushing pedestrian, the fastest being, I suppose, our minibus. On each side of the road traffic, moving in opposite directions, congealed into armies each squeezing past the other. Within these armies, fast vehicles like ours tended to get stuck in the tangle. It was of course impossible to squeeze by when passing traffic came in the opposite direction. All our driver could do was dash forward like a hussar when there was sufficient space between the two traffic armies, the road for a blessed half mile empty between them. Then he went all out for a bit until we caught up with the tail of the next slow-moving traffic army.

There was a strong sense of everything and everyone moving in straight lines across flat plains (or planes). Bicyclists, vans, lorries, buses, women walking along the roadside carrying hoes on their shoulders like rifles – all seemed directed by hidden purposes. And then there were of course the walls. Walls, just walls, walls sometimes into which houses seemed to have been inserted, with doors and windows gaping like mouths and eyes of a Humpty Dumpty face continuous with but above the level of a wall. Sometimes in villages spaces between houses had been filled with a crumbling mud or plaster wall or even a fence wall of yellow corn stalks. I asked Mr Lin why there were so many walls. He was in a doze induced by the rhythm of the minibus and seemed a bit startled by my question. He answered, waking with a start, 'Why, to protect people, of course.' 'Against what?' 'Oh, robbers, thieves, marauders.' Mentally, I switched all idea of such irregularities back into the past, the pre-Deng era, and had a sudden glimpse of war lords and their soldiers, perhaps the ragged rascals and robbers of the Cultural Revolution, torrents held back by walls.

With so many transportable objects – bricks, furniture, flagons, vegetables – heaped up on so many carts, the road made me think of an immigrating army coming one way, an emigrating army going the other way. What really impressed me was the sense of separateness and sameness – both at once – of individuals and groups. Everyone and every group had the air of carrying out instructions – to get somewhere, to convey something, to harvest the grain, to deliver some message, yet each seemed separate and alone. There was no shouting across the lines as there would have been, say, in Italy. Not on this road this morning anyway. Indeed, how unlike Italy, I thought, when our minibus almost ran into a man driving a cart. The man turned his head, looked at us with absolutely no expression on his face, seemed to take in the fact that we had not touched his vehicle or him, turned his head front-ways again and went on driving. The blasphemies that an Italian would have permitted himself on such an occasion seemed to print themselves silently on the air, like words coming out of a coarse mouth in a strip cartoon.

On our way, Mr Lin explained things to us which I copied down frantically in my note book, in handwriting slanting desperately against the sideways jerking movements of the minibus, trying to struggle through strangling traffic. Mr Lin was, in fact, an authoritative, intelligent, patient expounder of basic facts, extremely patient at answering questions, a careful listener and watchful of his own words in English, going back and correcting himself if he thought he had made a mistake. My notes went something like this:

The communes. Each commune ten villages. Production brigades. The workers' teams. People's councils. Committees. Attack on the countryside like that of an army, etc.

All the time I was telling myself I would be able anyway to look this up later. And later, we went to a communal farm and saw it all working (theoretically and ideally) under our eyes.

Mr Lin told us that some years back, as part of a scheme for breaking down barriers between town and country, he had been made to do agricultural labour. We looked at one another, unable to see him in this role. 'What did you do? Did you live in the country with a peasant family?' we asked, finding it difficult to imagine him shacked down in the straw. 'Oh no,' he said, 'I bicycled from Peking every morning, and back every night.' All, it seemed, with the utmost discipline and calm.

We passed fields, fields, fields, bright green, yellow, bare, dusty: flooded rice paddies that looked like mirrors reflecting sky pushed through by emerald spears, with peasants – surely the denizens of another age – wearing their sunflower straw hats and the women in their kirtled skirts stooped over the fields in fixed and silent postures like cranes with beaks downed, fishing in shallow waters. At intervals there were villages, quite varied: one, where the landscape was rolling, with shallow valleys, almost like a French village – houses scattered among hills – but most like encampments with huts, some of them of mud, and dirt paths running between houses. Towards the end of the journey we came to a town with buildings each side of the road, a roofed-in market with crowds going in and coming out busily and outside in the street peasants selling vegetables and livestock. This was different from Peking – even from what we had seen of the market there. Each salesman was busy promoting his wares. There was private enterprise. The people seemed also poorer and more traditional in their appearance than those in Peking.

At dinner back at the hotel that night, David picked on something I had said the previous morning to the poets: 'Yesterday you said to the poets that a difference between them and us was that they lived in a classless society. Actually, nothing could be further from the truth. There is more difference here between the peasants, who, we are told, form 80% of the population, and the townspeople than anything you'll find in England.'

We noticed that some inscriptions over the stores were in roman lettering. I asked Mr Lin why this was and he explained that there is a programme for romanizing Chinese characters. In addition to this, the characters themselves are being simplified, and the number reduced, decimated. As he talked I began to realize the great difficulties of carrying out such programmes. At present, he said, there are so many different dialects in China, that the *lingua franca* for people coming from remote areas is the characters. You see people meeting in towns who communicate by writing characters on pieces of paper. To write roman script for each separate dialect would not be the same thing. I thought it is as though Germans and English could communicate by a shared language of signs which indicated the same things, which they could not, of course, do if they merely wrote out words from their own languages in roman script.

Besides depriving the Chinese of a *lingua franca* of characters, romanization also means cutting them off from the immense heritage of their past literature written in those characters which are now to be reduced – so that an educated Chinese will need to know only three hundred instead of three thousand characters. But at what a price! The romanization is essential – one of the modernizations – but it means cutting tomorrow's China off from communication with the most accessible past of any civilization, in order to simplify its communication with wide areas of the modern world which is the present. As Mr Lin talked, I found myself wondering whether China's notorious reluctance to join the modern world, which had such disastrous political effects on it over the past two centuries, may not partly have been out of the desire to remain in contact with its own past civilization. Mr Lin seemed to think the process of romanization would be extremely slow.

We had lunch out of sandwich-boxes we brought with us which we took to a table in the section, special to tourists and foreigners, of a large restaurant near the tombs. To get there we walked through the central section of the restaurant, where there were Chinese. The din was tremendous, contradicting the impression I had received on the road of the Chinese going about their errands in complete silence – the silence of the man driving the cart whom we nearly ran into – which I find still more difficult to explain, having read, after this, of ear-splitting altercations between drivers and cyclists in Peking. The din in the main part of the restaurant made me wonder whether perhaps one reason why the authorities separate foreign visitors from the Chinese is because, if they were all of them together, the foreigners would not be able to hear themselves speak.

After lunch we walked along a road near the restaurant where there was a market for peasants to sell from stalls those precious few specimens of surplus produce which the people take everywhere to market (when they are allowed to). Despite the sparseness of their goods, there was an atmosphere of a bazaar about this little stretch of road, which could not have extended more than a hundred yards. David said: 'You see, they're happier here. They're hustling.'

*   *   *

It is impossible to comment on the Ch'ing Tombs. They were too vast, time was too short. We walked through immense courtyards and came to a great hall with wooden pillars and a long low roof at the top of steps which extended its whole length up to a platform on which there was a bronze crane and a bronze deer. Children took turns sitting on the back of the deer. We climbed up a square stone tower with ramparts on top of which there was another tower of brick – the stele tower – with two roofs one above the other, both upturned. From here we looked across the partly wooded plain to the mountains – the outline of which resembled chiselled curves, convex, the range semi-circular and distantly relating to the rectangles of the courtyards and ramparts, the roofs of halls and gateways and the main tower.

The same night, rather against our protests (I, tired and wanting to write my diary), we were taken by the ever-energetic Mr Lin to the Peking Opera. The opera house was large and bare and rather dark with rows of bucket seats close together. Most of the audience seemed to be of the older generation and there were, of course, many tourists.

I had expected a performance somewhat like Kabuki or the Noh drama, which I had seen in Tokyo. But it had little in common with these except a certain shrillness of the music, a lot of percussion and beating drums, rising to a fervid throbbing intensity at moments of climax. The music seemed to me like prolonged atonal recitative, occasionally becoming very rhythmic and with dramatic climaxes but not what I would have thought of as arias in which the music leaves behind what is being said to become the voice's pure melody or song. Although I did not, of course, understand the words – which are, we were told, declaimed in a very stylized way – the obvious great respect for language, whenever words were being spoken – as in fighting, dancing and acrobatic passages – and the music which was not purely orchestral, gave me the kind of pleasure I get from the language in Alban Berg's *Wozzeck*.

Although the stage effects are often pure melodrama, it struck me that there was a kind of calm at the centre of the performance – and of the music itself – the result of great control, stylization, symbolism, the classical effect which avoids realism even when the action is violent.

All the roles are conventional and type-cast, type-performed. Hero, heroine, old man, young man, warrior, priest, heroine's maid, demons, spirits, etc. Paint on faces and the lines in which they are daubed follow conventions which make it possible, I suppose, for the spectators of a Chinese opera to read the stage like a book with characters printed or written on it – most of them know it by heart. Paint on faces is so thick that it is like a skin-tight mask.

A young man, an eligible bachelor, it seems, meets a lady and her maidservant. The lady falls in love with the young man. They become engaged to be married. So much for the exposition, acted almost in pantomime, and with no great liveliness. After they are married, the young man sets himself up as an apothecary, and since his bride knows many magic arts, he does a thriving business. At this point an abbot announces to the young man that his wife is a snake – a real one, I mean, not metaphorical. Mr Lin is translating all this for me in whispers. I say to David, 'She turns into a snake. It is the plot of Keats' *Lamia*.' 'No,' counters David, 'just an ordinary marriage.'

When the young man has taken in the abbot's pronouncement, the opera suddenly becomes transformed into extraordinary life. The young man drops dead. But when I write drops, I mean he becomes completely rigid – as though rigor mortis has set in with the abbot's words. He hits the ground like a boomerang, bouncing up into the air and then falling back again, this time inert, surrounded by the lady and her maid who try in vain to revive him.

White Snake, who is immortal, returns to the heaven she came from, and restores her husband with a herb she has obtained there. He is not grateful and takes refuge from his wife with the Buddhist abbot at his monastery. I should not have related the story were it not for bringing it to the point where the action becomes completely magical, with a battle between the forces summoned by the White Snake and the abbot. The characters become demonic forces. The heroine, twisting and turning, and with coils of white muslin seething upwards from the bottom of her dress to her neck and almost enveloping her face, becomes entirely, outrageously, her own snake nature. Her maid, armed with a prong, becomes all demon. Demons and spirits from under the lake rush across the stage, dancing, turning cartwheels, juggling with darts and knives, wrestling. I am reminded of Japanese wood-engravings in which waves and spume take on the shapes of sheets of blue cloth with frayed white edges gyrating. In this battle of spirits and demons one looks into the forces of wind and water, a storm on the lake. Then White Snake, immortal but also a human wife married to an apothecary whom she is trying to save from the monastic life, becomes a wild creature hurling swords at a dragon who hurls them back at her. She catches them with her bare hands. She is a Fury. The dragon king duels with the water king.

Being alone without our two official guides each evening, at dinner, we exchanged impressions. Most of these altered daily, though we all three always agreed that the most obvious thing about China was that it had changed completely from what it had been early in the century. Everyone can see that it is no longer the China of coolies and rickshaws; women with bound feet; opium; war lords; civil war; Japanese occupation; exploitation by foreign imperialists; corruption of the Kuomintang; missionaries etc. It is a country where people can for the most part respect themselves and where they have at least the minimum standard of living which is necessary for self-respect. We realized though that in places we were not shown and which we would never see, there was still great poverty. Our guides did not exactly tell us this but they did not deny it either.

All the same, China did not give us any feeling of certainty about its future. There were too many unresolved conflicts for certainty: between left and right, the old and the younger generation, country and town.

David said he thought it was difficult, if not impossible, for China to attain communism because it had never been through the phase of industrialization under capitalism. Hence Mao Tse-tung tried to make it break through, in the Great Leap Forward, into communism without heavy industrialization, relying on the millions of the Chinese people to perform this miracle with their bare hands. Today, they were trying to increase industrialization through the encouragement – within limits – of free enterprise; but that might undermine the principle of communism.

Things about China made us think of school: the organization of everyone into groups, like classes, which were indoctrinated with the assumptions of the school: the certainty of the authorities that each member of the school must be fitted into the school's requirements, according to its curriculum.

Some years ago the authorities, in a moment of authoritarian over-confidence, decided that the children could be allowed to run their own magazine. They could trust them to express themselves without challenging the basic belief that all that really mattered to them were the principles on which the school was conducted and the survival of the school itself. The authorities felt that the exuberance of youth would perhaps restore to the school that spontaneity which bureaucrats lack. For a few heady months, self-expression, within these limits, was permitted. The dear old headmaster experienced in the blossoming of a hundred flowers the reflorescence of his own pioneering youth. But one day something terrible happened. A boy, sheltering under a pen name, published an article saying that another school, under a completely different system, was better than this one. There was an appalling row. The name of the boy who had written the article was quickly discovered, and he himself was expelled on the grounds that he was plotting to blow up the school. (In my room, I had been reading in the magazine *Index* about Wei Ching-sheng, author of *The Fifth Modernization – Democracy*, and of how he had been given a fifteen-year prison sentence for 'passing military secrets to foreign journalists'.) After this, publication of the school magazine was stopped. (Mr Lin had explained to us that Democracy Wall, on which people had been allowed to write up their opinions, had been abolished.) It was discovered that the headmaster, founder of the school, whose rules the children still obey, whose precepts are carved on some very expensive oak panelling in hall and corridors, whose sayings provide texts for sermons in the school chapel, was senile during the last years of his rule. One of his more eccentric acts was to give the children a year's holiday during which they were free to break the school windows, desecrate the sacred objects in the chapel, make the masters scrub floors and clean out lavatories, and, as a final insult, attend courses given them by their former pupils, become their teachers. That was the impression we had of the Cultural Revolution.

We discussed Mr Lin, our guide. He was a man of the world who had travelled to some extent, having worked in some capacity as a Chinese representative in Reykjavik for some years, and travelled to Denmark. He made it clear that he was a convinced communist. He was both proud and pleased to be an official. He never said anything that left the slightest doubt as to his political convictions, and he conveyed points of Chinese policy clearly, though not dogmatically. He translated for me a long article from the Peking newspaper showing that – within the limitations of Marxist-Leninist-Maoist thought – the party was taking an increasingly liberal attitude towards writers. When I asked him whether I could meet the novelist Ting Ling and a Chinese writer who had been a friend of mine in England during the Second World War and had returned to China after the revolution, he said he would make enquiries for me. Two days later, he reported back that he had done so, and that neither was in Peking. He seemed genuinely sorry about this.

Although we were shown only the places open to tourists, we were not stopped from photographing whatever we saw, which included some very poor people, peasants pushing or pulling carts loaded down with very heavy objects, back streets which were slums and houses in villages little better than hovels.

David said that one thing lacking in Chinese life was vicarious pleasure. No one enjoys simply the spectacle of others better off than himself making a show of their good fortune. The now elderly heads of government, in order not to excite envy, I suppose, look like undertakers trudging to their own graves, or being driven towards them in limousines like hearses.

The negative aspect of vicarious pleasure is envy. One looks at those better off and wishes they were worse off. One does this, I think, when it is impossible to see any connection between the conditions of one's own life and the lives of the more fortunate. The spectacle of another's enjoyment merely draws attention to one's own wretchedness. Envy can arise from a sense of social injustice and therefore express a yearning for justice. There are circumstances in which the conditions of a whole society might be based on the satisfaction of the envy of one social class for another.

Reading the newspapers, sometimes one has the impression that in China there is a licensed, institutionalized envy carried to ludicrous lengths. One reads about some official who, entertaining more exalted officials, goes to a good restaurant and orders an excellent meal, using the excuse of providing entertainment for superiors to satisfy his own greed. He is denounced and, in the bureaucratic equivalent of the game of Snakes and Ladders, descends to the tail of a snake. Necessary divisions in allotted tasks are interpreted as incipient class divisions. Managers of factories excite envy so they are made to work on the shop floor. Townspeople have advantages not shared by country people so they are sent into the country to do agricultural work (especially if they belong to that most easily envied class, the intellectuals). The Cultural Revolution was the most ferocious expression of the view that the high must be made low and the low made high: teachers must scrub floors and take lessons from their pupils. Envy is no longer of the poor for the rich, but of the stupid for the clever.

We talked about Chinese puritanism concerning sex, and thought that this was perhaps more apparent than real – an exercise in Chinese reticence. Later, we heard that in China there is an extensive sale of illicit pornographic literature.

The Chinese friend whom I had known during the Second World War, and who returned to China in 1949, has lived there ever since. However, I met him again recently in Europe, when he told me that the impression made on foreigners that the Chinese were puritanical was misleading. He added that in China, among men, friendship was the relationship that mattered most (without sexual implications). He said that usually Chinese men did not marry for love, but sometimes married couples did come to love each other later in life. (He may have been speaking for his own generation.)

25 May

We drove north-west to the Ming Tombs and thence to the Great Wall. The road from Peking goes over the plain for about twenty-eight miles until, just beyond a village called Chang Ping, there is a crossroads. The right-hand turning leads to the Ming Tombs in that beautifully cultivated, superbly civilized natural scenery where the mountains seem carved out of jade. They form a semi-circle like the tiered stone seats of a Greek theatre with the valley below, a stage, in which the thirteen imperial tombs, dating from the fourteenth to the seventeenth centuries, are distributed. The left-hand turning leads to the rugged mountainous country – stage scenery for invading hordes and roaming bandits, across which the Great Wall ferociously zigzags like a brindled serpent hissing at barbarians.

We took the right-hand turning to the Ming Tombs, seeing as we went the Ming Reservoir, constructed in 1958 (one of the good achievements, surely, of the Great Leap Forward – which Mao himself – if we were listening attentively to what Miss Li was telling us – took a hand in building). This sheet of water is like a mirror let into the landscape.

In attempting to describe later what we saw that morning, I am greatly indebted to Ann Paludan's book, *The Imperial Ming Tombs*, which has appeared since we left China. Reading it shows how much we missed during our brief visit. We did not, I think, stop at the magnificent Marble Gate – once part of a wall but now standing like a great sculptural screen with five narrow roofs at the roadside. There were once five wooden doors where there are now vertical oblong spaces – glassless windows – framing views of the green plain and the blue mountains outlined on the horizon.

We did stop at the Great Red Gate through which the road passes, providing a view of the Stele Pavilion, flanked by columns spreading out into brackets like wings which uplift the heavens.

The Stele Pavilion contains a gigantic tortoise, some six feet high and over fourteen feet in length, carved from a single stone and carrying saddled on its back a stele rising to a height of thirty feet. The tortoise has the embossed appearance of polished leather, even of bronze, so richly tooled and chased are its strange whiskers, scaly skin, segmented plated shell. Chinese animals in temple sculpture are by no means typical of their species. They have acquired characteristics of fabulous invented beasts. This tortoise is the one which features among the five symbolic animals of the ancient Chinese cosmology. It is also a very human tortoise, with upraised arched nose, lines like moustaches rippling backwards over bulging cheeks with dewlaps pulled back to the edge of the neck where the folds end in ornamental twisted points like the rays of the sun or the petals of a sunflower in an engraving by William Blake. With its raised head and eyes bulging like the cheeks, the tortoise looks a bit like an irate colonel having a snooze in an armchair at his club who, being suddenly wakened, stares indignantly across the top of his newspaper and across the room at an intruder.

We stopped to photograph Colonel Tortoise, then walked down the so-called Sacred Way (more accurately, the Way of the Spirit) towards the Tombs; this part of the approach road is lined with sculpted figures. We made halts at nearly every figure, first of pairs of animals, then of officials and warriors (one could scarcely call these 'humans'). The six animals featured, part real and part fabulous, are lion, hsieh-chai, camel, ch'i lin, elephant and horse: two of each, one standing and one seated. Supposedly they represent a round-the-clock watch over the dead, half of them on duty, the other half at rest waiting their turn.

The hsieh-chai is translated as 'unicorn' because it has a stiff top-knot of hair growing out of its forehead and laid back across its head. But it is a stolid, heavy, cloven-footed doggish and lionish chimera, nothing like the ivory-horned European unicorn.

David called the ch'i lin a griffin, but with its scaly hide, hair all drawn up to a point at the back of its head and dog-like face, it seems not quite vulturine. (When he got back to New York, David designed a model of it which he popped into his set for *Le Rossignol* at the Metropolitan Opera.)

The Sacred Way

The animals in the Sacred Way charm the visitors. One elephant peaceably rests the curved end of his trunk on the ground; another, kneeling, folds his legs, not under him, but so that the front feet are flexed outwards in front of his body, forming a cradle in that position in which his trunk rests. The horses are stolid, like fat ponies at the seaside waiting for children to ride them. The hsieh-chais and ch'i lins, fabulous beasts, have on their almost smiling faces the meekest, mildest expressions. The ancient sculptors gently tamed these beasts into becoming stone and they, in turn, tame the visitor.

After the animals, the Sacred Way bends in ritual fashion eastwards to evade evil spirits, which move in straight lines. We then come to the warrior figures, whose faces have the cruel impassive objectivity of functions they hold. Their chain of mail, batons, helmets and greaves, express a ferocity quite lacking in the fantasized animals. They are all authority, coarsely sculpted, rather boring. Children linger with the animals, ride astride their backs, but turn away from those men of power.

All the tombs (of which we only saw one) have very much the same layout, the only important difference being between the large ones which have three court-yards, and the small ones which have only two courtyards. In the case of those with three, and I quote here from Ann Paludan: 'there is a formal courtyard with three doors, then a courtyard leading to a Gate of Heavenly Favours. This . . . serves as a kind of porch – a place for receiving those who were going to perform the rites. It was through this gateway that the satisfied spirit would send good influences out to its living descendants – hence the name. The Gate of Heavenly Favours leads to a second courtyard on the far side of which stands the principal building, the Hall of Heavenly Favours . . . Behind the Hall of Heavenly Favours a doorway, often with three arches and decorated with glazed tiles, leads into the third court-yard, the north side of which is formed by a large stone tower on which stands the stele pavilion and by the crenellated ramparts surrounding the grave mound. There is also a protective screen door and a stone altar for sacrifices in the final courtyard.'

At the Ting Ling, the tomb of the Emperor Wan-li (1573–1620), we passed through two courtyards and across a terrace where the Court of Heavenly Favours had stood. In the third courtyard there were a great many trees and an altar on which there were five stone urns. We came to the entrance of the tomb, which was cut into the rampart wall surrounding the tumulus. Mr Lin told us of the rather extraordinary *Treasure Island*-like event which led to the discovery of the entrance to the tomb – indeed made it quite simple. Work was done on excavation from 1956 to 1958. The problem was to find the carefully concealed entrance in the wall built after the burial of the emperor in 1620. The workmen who had made the tomb were skilled in piling earth up over the actual tomb so that the entrance would be completely hidden. However, there was a place in the wall surrounding the tomb where the bricks were crumbling. The modern workers discovered here what seemed to be the entrance to the tomb, but after digging it out, they found a tunnel which was a dead end. Next they stumbled on a stele which had on it the words:

'The diamond wall begins 16 *chang* away and 3 *chang* down.' This was the entrance
they had been looking for, and with some ingenuity they managed to open the
marble doors that had been shut from inside in the interior of the tomb. They
found there the three coffins of the emperor and his two wives and a mass of
objects buried with them.

*Minibus and
warrior figure*

These objects have been removed and the coffins replaced by replicas. In a
central hall there are three marble thrones and stone urns. The Emperor Wan-li
who ascended the throne at the age of nine, in 1573, was, or rather became, a
deplorable character, unseen by his subjects: in the latter part of his reign, his
audiences with visitors consisted of their being led to his empty throne. Towards
the end of his life he was so fat that he was unable to move without assistance.

A crowd of Chinese stood in what we took to be awed silence in the hall where
the coffins were. David nudged me and said: 'They're worshipping their ancestors.'
After seeing the burial chambers we went outside into the daylight and climbed a
circular ramp, fortified with crenellated walls, to the terrace of the Square Tower,
above which stands the double-roofed stele tower. From there we had views of the
courtyards with their screens and altars and terraces, and huge trees each side,
below us, and the wonderfully peaceful landscape, to the north, fertile and partly
wooded and with foothills ascending to the semi-circle of protective mountains on
the skyline.

The Great Wall

When President Nixon was taken to the Great Wall he is reputed to have said: 'Gee, that's a great wall.' In some ways everything said about the Great Wall amounts to a variation on this. He might of course have done better to say: 'Gee, it's a great *old* wall', much of its appeal being that it is so ancient.

The American astronauts paid tribute when they said that the Great Wall was the only man-made construction on earth visible from the moon. The moon turns at once into a Chinese poem about the earth: it is a mirror which reflects one crooked scar running down the earth's physical features, the Chinese Great Wall.

The Wall was begun in the sixth century BC as separate sections to keep various warring states apart; these existing walls were linked up in the third century BC by the unifier of the empire, Shih Huang-ti (cf. Sian below): 300,000 men worked on it for ten years. Though so eminently visible, like a zigzag graph on a chart which everyone stares at to determine what it tells about the temperature of the world's oldest civilization, the Chinese Wall is more remarkable as an idea than as a beautiful or striking architectural object in itself. As pure abstraction, it is the apotheosis of the idea of China: it closes the world which is Chinese civilization upon itself, keeping out the barbarian.

A section of the Wall, that nearest to Peking, has been rebuilt and cleaned up, providing the most famous tourist attraction of China. Tourists arrive in thousands by train and in buses and charabancs and are deposited in an assembly and parking square with a few shed-like buildings attached where souvenirs are on sale. From here you can see the Wall like a giant chain with loops in it between pegs which are watch-towers, processional across the rugged mountains which look from here like a brown-green relief map of physical geography, with no special distinguishing features. One can imagine mounted barbarians, as rugged as the mountains, pouring down, a human tidal wave impeded only for a short time by the walls. Frontiers are fought for without anyone knowing quite where the frontiers are.

We climbed up steps leading from this parade ground of tourists to the nearby section of the Wall which swerved upwards between its two watch-towers – about half a mile apart, and went into the first of these which had a dark interior like a guardroom, and three arched windows. We walked out again and up a lot of steps to a second tower. The intrepid could walk to a third tower: and I have heard it said that some American professor and his son have walked the whole length of the Great Wall (or is it that they have endured the whole travail of the Long March?). So perhaps one could go on for ever, watched by the silence of the moon.

26 May   Sian (Xian)

At Peking airport we sat in the crammed aeroplane – a Russian turbo-prop Ilyushin – for half an hour before it took off. As, when the aeroplane was stationary, the air-conditioning did not function, we got incredibly hot. Altogether the heat is closing in on us. It will get worse the further south we go.

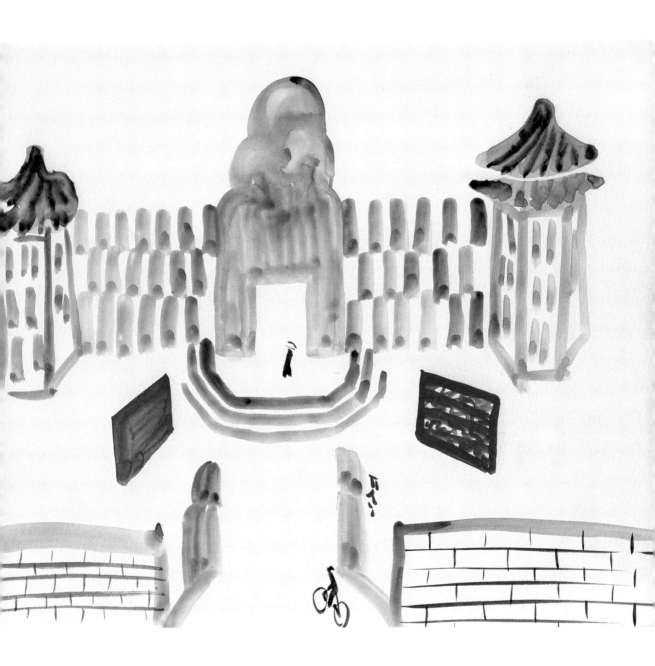

Hotel at Sian

On our arrival in Sian, it seemed much more Asian or at any rate Middle Eastern than Peking. We drove – in two cars this time – along a large dusty avenue with walls and rows of houses with wide pavements on either side, on which, at intervals, there were vendors of vegetables and a few other goods. Shops seemed to contain very few and rather tawdry objects. There were furniture stores and clothing stores (clothes are rationed).

Our hotel is an impressive concrete building five storeys high. It has a large entrance flanked by two small towers, and above the portico a projecting semi-circular shaft which goes up the height of all its floors and culminates above roof level in a tower. There is a large enclosed courtyard and driveway in front of the hotel.

The lobby is, as usual, crammed with tourists and luggage. Leading off from it there is a boutique with souvenirs, among them many lifeless paintings in the traditional style.

Under orders from Mr Lin, who set our timetable, we rushed up to our rooms, washed, did not unpack our luggage, came downstairs again and were introduced to our local guide, a bashful flower-like girl. We were piled into two cars and driven to the site of the Panpo village which a matriarchal clan inhabited in Neolithic times. They were followed later, the flower-like guide told us, by a patriarchal clan. There was a framed relief map of the area which had little red bulbs and little green bulbs on it. She pressed a button and the green bulbs lit up, indicating the habitations of the matriarchal clan; another button, and the red bulbs lit up indicating habitations of the patriarchal clan.

Bones and shards, relics of both clans, had been dug up in 1954. Archaeologists identified some of the stones as crude instruments for fashioning axe heads and arrow heads, tools for Stone-Age mass production. We peered through glass windows of showcases at exhibits demonstrating the evolution of the utensils, weapons and artefacts of the clans. After axe heads and arrow heads came vessels of clay, first of all pretty rough, but later developing into primal Abstract Art.

Above the cases containing these objects were oil paintings done in the style of academic Soviet socialist realism as taught at the Peking schools of art. These illustrated the lives of members of both clans, hunting and fishing until at last they reached that state of advancement where they started killing one another systematically. Swords have hilts which are engraved. A woman, kirtled and squatting, paints a cubistic fish on the side of a pot.

By this time the art displayed behind the glass windows has advanced so far that a jade fish-hook is worthy to be sold at Tiffany's. There are necklaces and girdles for women; holes made in shells lined with mother-of-pearl; teeth of wild animals, strung on leather thongs.

Next in a large showroom we saw huts progressing from holes dug in the ground to a circle of poles hammered into the earth with impacted mud walls between the poles and roofed over, with a hole as chimney in the roof. I imagined myself as a Neolithic man squatting on the mud floor of such a hut (there were no chairs) and

The Great Wild Goose Pagoda

extending the palms of my hands to a fire in the middle with smoke escaping through a hole in the roof, and the rain pouring down through the same hole and probably putting the fire out.

The most advanced dwellings were mud huts like those seen in villages in many parts of Asia, Africa and South America today. Primitive dwellings are dictated by necessity, I suppose, arriving at architecture which, without there being world communication, becomes world-wide. The modern international hippy retrogresses to the point where international Neolithic man weaves a mattress of leaves to sleep on and a rush mat to spread on the floor.

After the museum we came to the seven-storeyed Great Wild Goose Pagoda, part of a seventh-century Buddhist monastery. We passed through a gate which led to a large courtyard, at the end of which against a hedge, with the stone-coloured pagoda towering rather gloomy in the distance, there was a table with a vase of flowers and a solitary chair about a foot away, to one side. The top of the hedge was a light-yellowish green, with shadow below that. David took a photograph of what seemed very much a David Hockney arrangement.

We went into the garden that lay beyond the hedge and climbed some steps to the entrance of the pagoda. This was a Buddhist sanctuary with the particular quiet of Buddhist places – with its colour and smell of old stones and dark trees – emphasized, of course, by the fact that there were no Buddhists there. While David and Gregory climbed up the six flights of stairs of the Pagoda, I sat at the entrance on the ground floor with, seated beside me, an ancient custodian, wrinkle-faced, benign, calm, like some old retainer of an aristocratic household who remains in the same chair in the same place thirty years after the revolution which has driven out the aristocratic family.

27 May

David, who intended to look around the back streets of Sian this morning, postponed his walk when we learned that we were to go to the partly excavated burial mound of the first Ch'in Emperor, Shih Huang-ti, the tumulus under which a whole army of terracotta soldiers has been discovered. We were driven there in our two cars, David and Gregory in the first, Mr Lin and I in the second.

The drive was along a wide straight road lined on both sides with double rows of trees, across the plain, coloured yellow by the crops which were being harvested. Again the road was crowded with traffic – fast lorries and vans, slow horse-drawn carts, bicycles. All the work in the fields seemed to be done by hand, and apart from the occasional tractor, and trucks that were bearing away the harvest, we saw no agricultural machinery. One has the impression here of agriculture which has scarcely altered throughout the centuries. The peasants, with their lined, leathery, sun-furrowed faces, their straw hats, seem eternal, despite the very different conditions of their employment and their dazed, staring, shambling presence in museums and parks. We stopped at a place where there was a path leading from the

road across fields to a tumulus – one of the dozen or so in this district – in front of which there was a kind of concrete sentry-box with a little tiled roof over it. Some peasant women, gypsies, it seemed, were standing there selling straw handbags which had swastika patterns on them. We bought a few, thinking we might have done the same in Greece or Italy or Spain.

Then we drove on to the museum. It incorporates, under a hangar-like roof, an excavated section of a tumulus with part of the terracotta army whose members were unearthed in fragments – like broken dolls; although shattered, they were easy to reassemble so that the pieces could be glued together.

King Cheng Ch'in, in the north-western part of the country, commander of an army of a million men, was the first unifier and Emperor of China. In 211 BC he celebrated his conquest of all his enemies by taking the imperial name, Ch'in Shih Huang-ti, meaning 'the first Ch'in sovereign Emperor'. As well as being a conqueror, advised by his chief minister, Li Ssu, he was both a tyrant and a reformer. I quote from the introduction to the exhibition of some of the excavated statues held at Selfridges in London in April and May 1981:

On the advice of Li Ssu, feudal holdings were abolished and the nobles compelled to live in the West, away from their supporters. In the resettlement programme of 221 B.C. alone some 120,000 families were reported moved to Hsienyang, now the imperial capital. The peasantry received freehold rights on state property, and

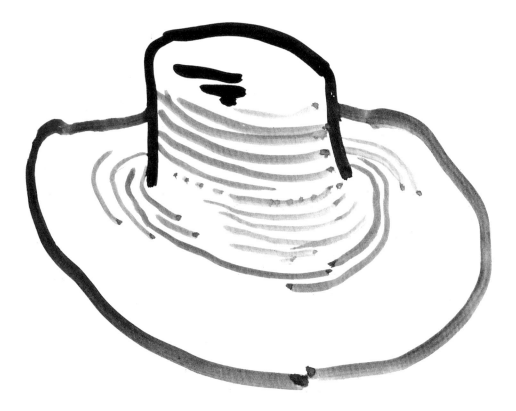

military service. The first Emperor also unified the laws and rules, weights and measures, and coinage. Against Li Ssu's instigation it was decreed that carts were all to be made equal gauge and that the characters used in writing were to be made uniform.

According to legends and folk songs the Emperor made himself extremely un-popular by conscripting people in hundreds of thousands to extend and complete the Great Wall, work on which was begun in 214 BC. Work on the tomb had already begun when the Emperor was still only king, in 246 BC. After he became Emperor the work was intensified and more than 700,000 conscripts were employed on supplying him with this posthumous army of terracotta models of more than life size officers and soldiers which presumably he would need in the next world. After the Emperor's death, the new Emperor, his son, piously decreed that all those of his concubines who were not mothers should be buried with him. Moreover it occurred to somebody that it would be prudent to bury with him all the artists and craftsmen who had worked on the tomb. This precaution was taken.

'Pit no. 1' has been excavated and the fragments of its contents pieced together. It contains 3,210 foot-soldiers, apart from officers and officials. Before entering this large area we went through halls in which various figures of men and horses were exhibited in glass cases. There were also spear heads and parts of other weapons (the wooden shafts have rotted away). One important official has, above his hat, which is closely fitted to his head, like a skull cap, a kind of pleated scarf in front. He has strong features with curling moustaches, wide eyes, and an imperious smile. Stalin would have fitted in well as generalissimo of this army. Another, more splendid, figure has a head-dress consisting of six bulging wads or panels of cloth, and a bow in front. It recalls the head-gear of the proud and arrogant youth de-picted in Bronzino's *Portrait of a Young Man* in the Metropolitan Museum, New York. These models tell you a great deal about the appearance and uniforms of their subjects. One supposes that the generals and top functionaries of such an army would look exactly like that, men who deliver orders but ask no questions.

The army is just an army of soldiers, most of them the same. One is reminded of tailors' dummies. Unlike the figures of the Parthenon frieze, they are not trans-figured with some vision of ideal beauty. The generals and high functionaries represent types of authority – nothing but authority – with enough in common with the Soviet leaders who are today photographed on the reviewing platform at some military display in Red Square to give them the stamp of repetition, reiteration. These then are the recurring constants of history.

People have been stunned by these discoveries, especially by the certainty that there are thousands, perhaps millions more such terracotta figures. China is numbers. Perhaps there are as many – no, far more – underground in terracotta as there are above in the flesh. Chinese archaeology has so far only scratched the surface of buried populations. They are impressive but also depressing, all too life-like in their mass. Certain figures, however, are enlivened by the artist's awareness. The horses have a moving, meek, stubborn passivity. The figure of a groom who

Guide in Sian

leads a horse reflects his feeling for the animal in his care. The gesture of an archer half-kneeling to tauten his cross-bow reveals the tension of the strain involved. This approaches the admiration realized in ancient Greek sculptures of hoplites.

Moving into the great shed or hangar, one sees trenches as wide as the lanes between the ramparts that surmount the Great Wall. The columns of soldiers march six men or four horses abreast. Standing on the platform overlooking these columns one has the overwhelming impression of figures marching relentlessly towards doom at the end of time. The faces express a determination consistent with the strength of the bodies – no ideal, or faith, or fanaticism – just impersonal strength, and discipline. Looking at them one can well be thankful not to have been born in their time, place and generation.

They remind us of terrible things done by armies in our own day, but they are also a formidable resurrection of the past: as though the names of armies in their hosts in the Old Testament suddenly became models of their bearers. They strike one with their reality like the bodies moulded for posterity in the falling ash of Pompeii or the victims of Hiroshima. They evoke their civilization in a way which makes us ask what ours would consist of if preserved in perfect replica two thousand years hence and what people would think then of its roads channelled between skyscrapers, its machines and its figures like tailors' dummies.

We had luncheon at a restaurant in Sian – in an upstairs room reserved for foreigners, with separate tables for groups of tourists. It was a large, light, airy, rather pleasant room. Our pretty local guide, while we were still sitting at table, asked David to do a drawing of her, which he obligingly did. Within a few minutes the waiter at our table stopped serving (there was a group of French tourists at the next table who seemed to be left unattended) and was standing over David watching the progress of his work. Soon other waiters appeared and, after them, sweating and smiling, the chef. David finished his drawing. He then fished into the enormous canvas bag which Gregory always carried round and drew out his Polaroid camera. He took the guide across the dining room to a window and photographed her, setting down the portrait he had just done, on another chair beside her, for comparison. By now the whole staff of the restaurant – or of the foreigners' section of it

– was clustered by the window. David took a charming photograph of the chef –
wearing his white chef's cap – flanked by two assistants.

After this, even outside the restaurant in the street, where there was a small
crowd awaiting us, the citizens of Sian seemed particularly friendly, as though we
were three Goons arrived there. We did look rather funny: David with the flat cap
he nearly always wears, even indoors, his shirt with horizontal red stripes and his
different coloured socks; Gregory with his Robin Hood jerkin with a kind of cape
at the back; and me with my enormous feet. The Chinese, I noticed, were always
looking at my feet and politely concealing their smiles.

We went to the Great Mosque which, Nagel's Guide tells us, is the largest of
fourteen mosques said still to be in use in Sian. It is 'in the middle of a district
chiefly inhabited by Hui Minority people . . . and was founded in AD 742. The
present buildings', the Guide goes on, 'date mainly from the end of the 14th century.' The Mosque has been restored several times. It is a particularly charming
place, a mixture of styles, with Chinese features superimposed on the more familiar
Islamic style of mosques in the Middle East.

It is in a narrow street of small houses with roofs of old tiles and plastered walls
on which telephone poles with slack wires weave spidery shadows. We entered a
courtyard through a door which was in no way remarkable. A high stele of phallic

shape and proportions stands at one end of the courtyard which contains a leafy, shrubby garden with paths in an oblong round it and rather humble hut-like buildings, and at the other end a small pagoda with three tiers of roofs. There is a further courtyard with a garden consisting of plants in pots or in circular beds cut in the paving, each of them separate like the magnified forms of first snowflakes on a slate. There are more steles, some of them elaborately carved. At the end we came to a low building with a long roof supported on columns at intervals along its whole length. Passing through a stone archway and entering this building, across a bare plain courtyard, we suddenly saw the point of its being Moslem. In a huge carpeted space men and women, separate as those plants outside in the courtyard, kneel on carpets and bow their heads to the ground in prayer.

The mosque seemed to have quite a congregation because as we were leaving we saw a great many people coming in, most of them wearing fezes. Strange, the contrast between this solemn area of quiet and prayer and the completely Chinese character of the courtyards.

We went back into the charming narrow street with its steeply roofed single-storey houses and plastered walls like some old quarter in Morocco, or a painting of Montmartre by Utrillo. Little boys came running towards us. When we stopped they stood around scratching the palms of their left hands with their right ones, calling out the shrill, street-Arab-like word, 'payn'. I felt rather nervous, thinking they meant 'penny' and that if we gave them money we might get them into trouble (one is told there are no beggars in China). Gregory quietly ascertained that what they were really saying was 'pen'. They sought from tourists ballpoint pens, one of the magical consumer-goods items much lusted for by the young. 'To do their examinations with', said Mr Lin piously. But we also heard one whisper, *sotto voce*, 'cigarettes?'

We got back to the hotel at the miraculously early hour of 2.30 p.m. Then I slept for an hour and woke up feeling extremely tired and with a panicky reaction: 'I should never have let myself rest during the day until this trip is over.'

We had dinner at the hotel. Then, being alone, we seized on the opportunity to take a longish walk through the part of Sian nearby. The width of the streets and the trees along them give Sian, especially at night, the air of some former French colonial city such as Casablanca. One half expects to see tables outside cafés. There are none.

We passed a man pushing a cart carrying an open container of shit giving off a smell so pungent it seemed to cut through us. We crossed the street to avoid this odour and found ourselves in a street of houses – hovels almost. The whole breadth of a house would be about twelve feet, we reckoned. As we walked along, David told us about the shit carrier in an East Yorkshire village where he went harvesting when he was a youth. The village was called Wetwang. 'And there was this old man called Tommy Jackson. All the labourers used to eat with the foreman, in his house. There were eight of us in all. Tommy Jackson who was one of us used to clean out the lavatory cans by hand, very rough big hands he had. He never took a bath – ever – he had never been known to be in a bath in his life – his hands were always filthy. When we were having dinner, the gravy was in a bowl. One day someone asked him to pass the bowl and he showed his big hand covered with dirt right into the gravy. After that, people used to say, "Don't you bother, Tommy." '

I remarked that China was not as scrupulously clean as Japan – the various lakes, pools and rivulets in temples we have visited have wrappings from ice cream etc. in them – touristic detritus – but, on the other hand, it was not as dirty as America – and I remembered the grounds of the Chicago zoo covered with marshmallows scattered all over the grass like puff balls. David thought that probably in ten years' time things would look far far better in China.

We came to another main street and peered into shops: shirts, a few suits, a woman's dress. David said: 'Well, I think that in the 1930s a clothing store in a French provincial town wouldn't have looked much better than this.'

A little further along the road there was a crowd of people watching a cripple who was banging a metal plate loudly against the pavement. He had one foot twisted backwards behind his whole back so that the foot clasped his neck. He removed the foot from this position and with his hands forced his twisted legs in front of him. Then he brought his hands down to the pavement and started hopping on them as though they were feet and he a hideous maimed bird. There was a touch of medieval Europe about this, of Victor Hugo's *Notre Dame de Paris*. I thought: 'So far this is the only beggar we have seen in China, but then we haven't before this ever walked about the streets alone. And two-thirds of China is not open to be seen by foreigners.'

While we were lingering, a youngish man, tall and with an intent expression, asked us whether we were English. 'One American and two English,' David said. Questioning and answering followed, about where we came from and what we did. A frizzy-haired girl pushing a bicycle by the young man's side was, he told us, his girlfriend. He said he was studying English at the university. I asked him whether he liked Sian and he said no, he didn't; as a city it was boring and noisy. He would like to go to Peking or Shanghai. I remarked: 'Shanghai must be still noisier.' He said: 'Yes, but . . .', as though the noise of Shanghai would somehow be better than that of Sian. I asked him what he studied at the university. He said Shakespeare, but it was very difficult. Even his professors did not understand many things in it, in spite of the fact that some of them were Americans. (Several Chinese students we met seemed to feel about Shakespeare as boys in Dickens do about their ancient enemies the Romans.) 'Sometimes we don't understand, and we're English', said David. The young man asked whether, if he gave us Chinese money, we would go into the Friendship Store (Friendship Stores are exclusively for foreigners) and buy him some cigarettes with what he called our 'funny money' (he meant Chinese paper currency specifically issued for foreigners). It so happened that none of us had money on him. David said that if he walked with us to the hotel, Gregory would run upstairs and get some money with which he could buy cigarettes at the hotel. On our way there, the young man said: 'Well, if you could change some more of my Chinese money for your funny money I could buy my girlfriend a skirt in the Friendship Store.' We let this pass unheeded. We came to the hotel and David and I stood outside while Gregory went inside for the money. 'Perhaps you had better leave me and go in with him and come back and meet me later', said the young man, 'because if you stay here there will soon be a crowd', and sure enough, even as he spoke, young people were appearing out of the darkness from everywhere, and asking: 'Are you English?' We went into the hotel (where the Chinese were not allowed to enter) and later David took three packets of cigarettes out to the young man. David said that to people standing out there on the kerb, the life inside this hotel must seem as exotic and glamorous as that inside the Ritz would be to a news vendor in Piccadilly.

28 May Nanking (Nanjing)

In accordance with instructions given us by Mr Lin, we got up at 5 a.m. at Sian, breakfasted at 6 and took an aeroplane at 7 to Nanking. Driving to the airport, I noticed how beautifully they've planted the streets nearby with a line of Chinese poplars and behind them a line of cypresses.

The plane was again Russian, a bit more old-fashioned than the Ilyushin to Sian, it seemed, with bucket seats. We flew over flat country, bright green and golden with the growing crops.

At Sian airport I had noticed a young, very obviously English couple, both of them about nineteen years old. At an intermediate stop between Sian and Nanking we got into conversation. He was in that interval of life between school and university, and was going to Cambridge. She, also having just left school, was going to Oxford. He would read law, she English. He told me that they had travelled across Russia to the Chinese border. Simon and Janet (those were their names) had joined a tourist group of eleven people through Russia and a different, and larger, group through China. He said they had found the Russians very friendly. The Russians seemed depressed about politics and did not want to discuss them. However, the leader of their group in Russia had herself broached the subject of Afghanistan and put across the party line: that under the terms of some treaty, and in answer to the appeal of the Afghanistan government, the Russians had moved in to assist a friendly power.

We were much taken with Nanking, the old southern capital, with its wide tree-lined avenues and streets crossing them at right-angles. There are plane trees (first brought from France in the early 1930s) and Himalayan pines. Our local guide, a rather squat, jolly looking girl to whom, I fear, we did not pay enough attention, produced the usual columns of statistics. Since 1959 the people of China have planted 32 million trees. There is an annual 'tree day' in Nanking when new trees are planted. Since 1959 some 200,000 trees have been planted there.

On reflection, this makes sense of what a friend of mine, referring to China, said: 'That birdless, treeless country.' Once, when we saw a bird, Mr Lin admitted that this was a rare sight and that the Chinese have killed almost all the birds in their country. During the Cultural Revolution trees were cut down recklessly for fuel. What one comes back to always in China is that there are millions of people, millions of soldiers alive, millions of clay models of soldiers still waiting to be dug up, millions of Chinese waiting to plant millions of trees. If every Chinese could produce a bird's egg there would be millions of birds.

Nanking, at any rate, is a city of trees, especially of plane trees – reminding me of that tree-tunnelled city, Aix-en-Provence. There are also more goods to be seen in the shops than in Sian. There isn't the feeling here of great bare dust-blown acres which give Peking's buildings the appearance of columns of tanks lined up in a desert. So far, our impressions of Nanking have been of long avenues with large tenements and public buildings either side, or long walls, crowded with people who, as David remarked, do not look like Party members.

Simon and Janet joined us sightseeing. They were pleased to get away from the tourist party to which they were attached. As we were in the car together I questioned Simon further on their trip to Russia. He thought that despite their disputes, Russian and Chinese political jargon was very similar. (Occasionally I had the impression during our stay that China has caught Russian communism like a terminal disease which no one wants to mention: the Party, the architecture, the communal farms, the educational system, the press, the artists' union, the writers' union, the whole lot.) Under the official attitudes in Russia, Simon had felt there was a very deep disillusionment with politics (in China one sometimes feels, I thought, that politics has become like sleep-walking). Simon said that yesterday evening, in Sian, Janet and he had started talking to some young people who came up to them (exactly as young people had done in Russia), and then invited them up to their apartment. Several other young people had joined them there. The apartment consisted of a very small kitchen, to the right of the entrance, a small living room, whose principal piece of furniture was a TV set, and a bedroom with two beds in it. Simon, who, I think, more than his friend Janet, tends to judge things by the standards of his English home and school, described the apartment as 'squalid'. David remarked later that many people in England live in conditions no better than these.

Simon's and Janet's hosts told them that they were completely bored with politics. They said that they had no prospect of getting jobs and that people in the country were even worse off than they. One student had a collection of banknotes from various countries, which he had shown them. Simon produced an English note, something none of them had ever seen before. Their collector friend asked if he could buy this for whatever it might be worth in yuan. Simon said he would be very happy to give it to him. Their host then said that he would like to present Simon, as a souvenir, with an object which had been given him by his grandmother and to which, as a child, he had attached great sentimental value, but which he would now be very glad to get rid of. It was a medallion of Chairman Mao.

The conversation which Simon reported to us may of course be of little significance. For, given the disfavour with which the authorities regard Chinese who want to meet foreigners unofficially, only the most disgruntled and therefore undesirable 'elements' make the effort to converse with strangers. But of course it is not just that the authorities distrust their own people. It is also that they wish to prevent the foreign tourists from gaining unfavourable impressions through unscheduled meetings with the Chinese. In socialist countries, when and where tourism is permitted, the authorities cannot resist the temptation to make it – perhaps simply through nothing more sinister than force of habit – an exercise in brain-washing the visitor. What one likes about the Chinese, even the guides and officials, is that they seem rather to want to have real discussions about things and are half-hearted about telling lies. They do not tell more than they are allowed to, but they are not cynical and they are often apologetic. As the poets we met in Peking had told us, during the Cultural Revolution they did not write about certain themes simply because they were not allowed to do so. I had the impression that there is much natural goodwill and friendliness among the Chinese. They would like you to understand that if they do not discuss politics in China beyond a certain area of permitted topics this is not because they do not wish to do so but because – and they wish you to believe this – discussion of certain things is not allowed.

Simon and Janet went with us to see that feat of engineering, pride of Nanking, the road and rail bridge across the Yangtze river. On each side, long before the central span which actually crosses the river, the bridge traverses the partly industrial, partly agricultural landscape. When you approach the central span you are greeted by immensely high concrete statues of revolutionary figures with upraised arms, leaning forward and facing you in a challenging manner. At the end of the bridge nearest the city there is a building like a large kiosk with a reception

room where chairs are placed opposite a scale-model of the bridge, boxed in a long shallow glass case. There is also a lobby with a statue of Mao Tse-tung dressed in his usual dungarees, and with one arm rather informally raised. We were given tea, as usual, and informed by a guide as to the bridge's vital statistics: built between 1960 and 1968, it has four piers and is the longest bridge in China – over 4,500 m (4,900 yds); 5,000 workers were employed in its construction, using a million tons of concrete. After this talk we were taken by lift to an observation tower from which

展場内请勿拍照、吸烟

NO SMOKING !
NO PICTURE !

館内で写真さつえいと喫煙
はご遠慮ください

we looked out across the great mud-coloured river with strings of barges moving on it. The bridge itself dissected the view: on one side long brown and orange fields could be seen receding into the horizon like the sections of a fan spread out; on the other rugged fields and some trees and beyond them the outline of mountains against the sky. Behind us was the town, humped and smoky.

On the wide observation platform where we stood there was a group of Japanese nuns in black and with close-cropped hair, wrinkled faces grinning at us benignly, a bit absurd, but lovable. In a People's Republic any evidence of religion brings with it a spiritual savour like incense. David described to me his feelings on hearing Dvořák's Mass in the cathedral of Prague in 1970. He said: 'The congregation was as intensely a choir of the spirit as the actual choir was of the music.'

We drove back towards the far end of the bridge where we got out and saw another view, then turned back to the town where we alighted at the Drum Tower. It looks like the body of a windmill without sails and is painted carmine. It is the sole remaining pediment of an ancient palace, built in 1382. In the ground-floor rooms there was an exhibition of paintings by a 36-year-old painter called Wu Yue-shi, who, we were told, began painting when he was eight. They were freely and freshly painted works in ink or in watercolour on mostly traditional themes – mountains, rocks, trees, birds, flowers, villages, huts, figures – but treated with

GE and scale-model of bridge

97

freedom and with original observation. Some had patches of colour and inscriptions written across or down the sides covering with calligraphy a large area of the work. David admired this painter's awareness of the medium he was using in each picture and his loose handling of his subjects. I tried to buy one. I was told that the artist was in Peking and, although the pictures were for sale, this made it difficult.

We were then taken off to the museum of the Heavenly Kingdom of Great Peace which is situated in the palace of the Eastern Lord, Yang Hsin-ching, with its three great halls and garden. The museum is a good example of the way in which, seen with the hindsight of their revolution, the Chinese present past history as leading to the apotheosis of the Chinese Republic. The main theme illustrated here is the Taiping rising. There are photographs, maps, a proclamation by Hong Hsiu Chu'uan denouncing the Manchu rulers, seals, coins, cannon balls, etc.

Janet went with David and Gregory and the lady interpreter in one car, Mr Lin, Simon and I in the other. During the ride from the Yangtze bridge to the Drum Tower, Simon suddenly started displaying forensic skill in submitting Mr Lin to a severe cross-examination. He began by asking Mr Lin whether it was possible to see the famous wall-posters in Peking. Mr Lin said firmly no, it was no longer possible because they no longer existed. 'Why is that,' asked Simon, following up before Mr Lin had time to answer with 'Does it mean that the right to criticize has been abolished?' 'Not at all,' said Mr Lin a bit stiffly, 'criticism can and does continue to take place, but through the proper channels.' 'And what are they?' 'The newspapers. Readers who wish to criticize may write to the newspapers.' 'But the editors of the newspapers, who choose the letters, are themselves government employees and reflect the views of the government.' 'Not at all,' said Mr Lin, 'the newspapers contain many letters from readers which are highly critical.'

There was a pause, then Simon started off on another line of attack: 'What about minority views? Supposing that a member of some minority writes expressing his desire for the freedom of that minority?' Mr Lin became cautious: 'He may do so, of course. A majority may grow out of a minority. But no minority can develop itself into a majority if it does not represent the truth.' After this proposition of doubtful logic, Mr Lin added: 'Though readers are free to write whatever they choose, naturally an editor would not publish a letter which put forward some preposterous view, such as that it was necessary to eat ten or twenty meals a day.'

Mr Lin and Simon sat in the back of the car. I was in front – on account of the extra space claimed by groggy knees – beside the driver and had the detachment from their conversation like that of a member of the audience from two boxers in the ring. I felt grateful that Simon was asking questions I myself would never have asked because I already knew the kind of answers which Mr Lin was bound to give. There seemed to me something humiliating about asking someone a question to which he cannot do other than give an official Party line answer, and I tended to avoid doing so. On the other hand, not to ask is also a bit insulting, because it assumes that the person asked does not have an opinion of his own. Not to ask also makes one a bad reporter.

Mr Lin said in answer to some further question from Simon about the freedom of the minority: 'Today in China a tiny minority opposes the will of the people, which the government represents. The government accepts criticism within the context of Marxist-Leninist-Maoist thought but it cannot accept opposition outside that, because to do so would be against the interest of the people.'

When we reached the exhibition at the Drum Tower which I have already described, I managed to draw aside first Simon and later Mr Lin. I said to Simon: 'I agree in general with your attitude, but I don't think that the logic of your argument about freedom of speech applies in all circumstances absolutely. A revolution which is based on the transference of power from one social class to another cannot afford to let the opposition speak until the principles of the revolution have become accepted by the whole society. Capitalism can afford to let the opposition speak because such extremely strong forces in the society back its ideology and its ruling class. But if a socialist revolution allows those who wish to destroy its freedom to oppose the basic ideology of the revolution, it slumps back into representing the interest of the class it has overthrown. Look at what has happened to all the social democratic parties in Europe which really do not support socialism at all.'

I was not sure whether I myself agreed with these arguments I was expounding. They were in fact opinions I do not hold but sometimes use against myself. I was trying to make him understand that the point of view which Mr Lin was putting forward was not based simply on bad faith, as Simon appeared to think. Simon looked thoughtful and, I suppose, labelled me in his mind as an apologist for communism.

Later, when I had an opportunity to be alone with him, I said to Mr Lin: 'Of course, I understand your argument that you cannot at this stage of the revolution permit the voice of real opposition. To my mind, though, the danger of crushing all real opposition is that a government which does so, having made itself irremovable, may then make terrible mistakes. The tragedy of intellectuals I have known in Eastern Europe is that, having recognized the sacrifice of their own individual freedom as being politically necessary, they gladly sacrificed their right to oppose communism on the grounds that their opposition was individualist self-indulgence, but subsequently found that they had to stand aside helpless when the government to which they made the sacrifice of their individual freedom committed frightful injustices. What they earlier regarded as their bourgeois right to express personal whims, a pampered luxury, is suddenly seen by them as the truth that must be spoken in order to prevent murders, torture, concentration camps for thousands, including many members of the "masses". They realize then that, in the name of the people, they have sacrificed their right to save the people.'

Mr Lin said: 'I understand your point of view very well. In China today we think democratic centralism is very essential. We go in for criticizing the party leadership, and if the leadership neglects this criticism things might go wrong. Actually, in the last years we had some set-backs in our work, and one of the reasons for this was that the leadership, in some respects, neglected criticism.'

29 May

We were taken to a pleasant house, situated in a public garden, which belongs to the Nanking Institute of Calligraphy and Painting. We were received by about a dozen artists, none of them very young. The oldest had a monkish skull-like face, lined but with an eager expression, rather beautiful. He watched and listened as though things were a bit remote for him. There were two younger painters, one of them bespectacled with twinkling eyes behind lenses; another bristle-haired, tough, warm; two official-looking types seemingly very conscious of their responsibilities. The impression was of a smiling team.

On the walls hung examples of their art. Some of the calligraphy consisted of angular modernist ideograms. I remarked to David, while we were looking at these, that to a Chinese each ideogram is like a musical scale, or a pattern of given notes on which a composer may make variations within the chosen key. He agreed and said, 'And it's possible to put every kind of expression into the characters in ideograms, even humour, to make them look funny,' pointing to a text in which this was done. The pictures covered a limited range of themes: mountains, waterfalls, bamboos, boats, flowers, birds, insects. One had the impression there was a more modern freedom in doing the ideograms than the paintings.

While we sat facing the pictures on the walls opposite us, we were given the usual cups of tea. The director, Mr Tsao Wen, with his colleagues in a semi-circle around him, began by saying that the Institute was set up in 1979. It had been planned to begin long before this, but progress had been impeded by the machinations of the Gang of Four. Nanking, he went on to say, was a city of old culture, distinguished especially in calligraphy and painting. In the past, many famous painters from other cities had come to visit their colleagues in Nanking. So, after the Liberation, under the guidance of the Party, painting and calligraphy were able to extend their development. The famous painter Fu Pao-shi lived and worked here. His influence in this area among his contemporaries was very great and extended to later painters; he died in 1965 at the age of 61.

He mentioned the name of famous calligraphers who in 1956 joined what was then the Research Association of Chinese Painting in Nanking and who died during the Cultural Revolution. Those still surviving were Li Chen-tsai and Hsiao Hsian who learned her art from Huang Pin-hong, whose most intense period of activity was the end of the Ching dynasty and who died in 1950 at the age of 90. (One had the weird feeling of being almost in a company of ghosts from the past, producing their traditional art, but who, after all, had survived the unleashed hippies of the Cultural Revolution.)

The director went on with his serious discourse. There are, he said, many poems on calligraphy written by one who was himself a calligrapher, Lin San-chi. Here is one:

When you write you'll write in a curving script: but actually the purpose of this script is to write very straight. And when you draw a circle you are actually in search of a square. I wish very much to offer this concept to my colleagues who learn calligraphy.

We seemed in contact with a China older than any we had come across so far.

Another of his poems, the director went on to say, runs:

When you have entirely overturned the ink from your inkwell then you will be as famous a calligrapher as were Zhung and Wang.

(I puzzle over this, wondering whether by 'overturned' is not meant 'exhausted', but preferring 'overturned'.)

David, who was looking rather green, having been up five times during the night with the 'runs', here murmured: 'The poetry is the subject of the poem.'

The director now moved on from the subject of the poems written by calligraphers about calligraphy to mention more general principles: 'When you paint you must not restrict yourself to the object. You must go beyond the object and in this way realize your own feelings about it. . . . A fundamental principle of Chinese painting is that you can end the painting but your feelings will be endless.'

I thought of citing Paul Valéry's much-quoted dictum, that a poem is never finished, but abandoned. Looking round the room at their pictures and their calligraphy and their painting, I thought how far this seemed from communism, and how near to the ambiguous pronouncements in Goethe's *West-Östlicher Divan*. Although very sympathetic and with a feeling that we were all among colleagues, flattering to us visitors, the company was not young or new.

The last example of calligraphy shown to us was by the woman calligrapher Hsiao Hsian. It was certainly very striking and seemed to be one the members of the Association were particularly proud of. It consisted of very bold brushwork in thick strong black strokes and was, we were told, done in celebration of the thirtieth anniversary of the Republic. Squeezed into English it yielded a message rather like some political aphorism from Ezra Pound's *Cantos*:

MODERNIZATION GROUNDWORK FOR 1000 YEARS DURING LAST 30 YEARS WE HAVE UNIFIED MOTHERLAND

Ezra Pound – who derived the idea from Fenollosa – argued that Chinese characters conveyed at one and the same time the meaning of words and their visualized compressed poetic images. The experts say this is not so; and indeed, I can hardly believe that in reading a Chinese newspaper the reader has a mental visual newsreel of the events about which he is reading, conveyed by characters. What is true, however, is that the calligrapher who writes a poem which is also a work of visual art as characters creates a work which combines two qualities independent of – but perhaps complementary to – each other: one the verbal meaning, the other the calligraphy itself.

The artists then showed us some of their paintings. Each, turning towards us, bowing slightly, smiling shyly, produced a painting. Then, at David's request, they showed us the tools of their trade, brushes, inks and watercolour. David was feeling too ill to try them himself. They then painted collectively two pictures – one for David and one for me (six participated in the one for David, two in the one for me). David watched closely the way in which they used their brushes – with little medium on them and making marks which imprint on the paper the part of the brush used: the tip, or the full brush or a trident of marks resulting from splaying the hairs of the brush out with gaps between hairs. Each brush had as it were its vocabulary of signs it could employ. They painted themes that seemed a bit predictable: the falling straight and curved lines of water, the rocks from which it falls, trees on either side, the irregular platform-like landscape in the foreground, huts, etc. That was the picture for David; for me, a bough with plums on it done by one artist, and two birds flying underneath it done by another.

While each artist worked, the others stood round him watching, breathless almost, as though he were a juggler balancing shapes, though all the while afraid that some stroke might be out of balance and the whole arrangement tumble. As the accumulations of rocks, water, trees, bamboo, became more crowded the danger of a false move, toppling the balance of the whole, became greater. It was a relief when the last of the artists working on David's picture, the drawing in ink being completed, began the more relaxed task of filling it in with patches of colour – orange ochre, emerald green and indigo blue.

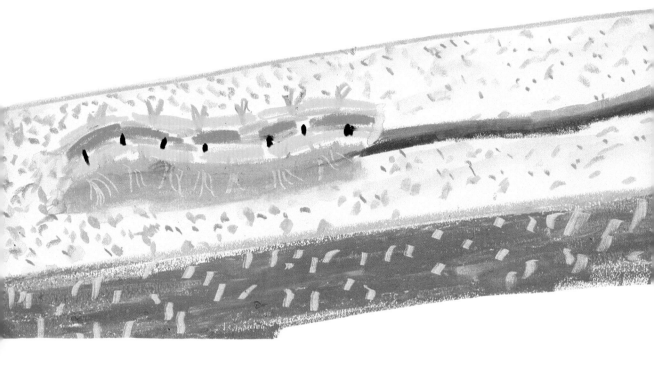

Although David had been feeling too ill to paint together with them, there was a very good feeling about this meeting of a kind that occurs between dedicated artists, a sense – since we were brought together for so short a time and came from such different places and forms of society – of honouring the occasion – of *Ave atque Vale*, hail and farewell. I wondered whether calligraphers would ever interweave characters – ideograms – superimpose them on one another, fuse them, making identical things opposite, whether there is a composite character meaning hail/ farewell cancelling geography and ideology – leaping over and ignoring our repulsive political systems – with friendship.

David went straight back to the hotel and to bed for the rest of the day. Gregory and I were taken by Mr Lin and the local guide first to Kuan Wu, a large lake where there are five little islands and thousands of willow trees, and then to the nearby zoo where we saw two peacocks spreading their tails before delighted spectators. When we were there, the panda was asleep. Close to us, on the grass, there sat and lay a group of children – in the surprisingly gay clothes children wear in China – spread out, many-coloured like those peacocks' tails. Their schoolmistress, who stood up above them like that peacock's head and beak, ordered them to sleep. All, or nearly all, shut their eyes and were asleep in an instant like the snapping of a lock. One or two little legs or arms remained vertical and were gently pushed into the horizontal by the schoolmistress.

In the afternoon, Gregory and I and Mr Lin went to the Sun Yat-sen Mausoleum, the construction of which began in 1925 and was completed in 1929. To reach this massive pretentious building with its azure-tiled roof, and the statue of Sun Yat-sen looking solemn and dedicated, you have to climb 392 steps. I let Gregory climb them while I sat on one of the rare benches which the People's Republic provides at memorials, and watched another little troop of children. This time they were playing a game in which, while the rest sat down in a circle, one of them had to run round the others and, before he or she was allowed to sit down in the circle, sing a little song. I think no one would dispute that Chinese children provide a rare glimpse of a world of perfect manners, gaiety, charm, colour, happiness. Watching them, I wondered whether the Chinese do not experience some sense of the vicarious in life in watching their children. To the visitor, seeing them at play is the most delightful of many mysteries this poetic country provides.

Other things we saw on that busy day in Nanking are vague in my mind: a modern pagoda; a vast house in a wood where Madame Chiang Kai-shek lived from 1946 to 1949. It is now a tea room and a very gloomy shopping store for souvenirs, jade etc. We went to another Sacred Way with stone figures of horses, lions, camels, chimeras, similar to the one we had seen on our way to the Ming Tombs. An artist was seated at the edge of the road, which is about a third the width of the Sacred Way, doing a sketch in the style of Western Impressionist painting. From this, and the elegant attire of the girl with him, I gathered he must be an Overseas Chinese. In a meadow nearby, soldiers were exercising marching back and forth, doing the goose step.

30 May   Hangchow (Hangzhou)

The drive from Nanking to Hangchow very beautiful. First along the highway through fields that looked a richer orange and a more brilliant green than those we had driven through further north. There were paddy fields with peasants stooped over their work. From the car, peasants standing in fields of grain seemed, against the light, like their own shadows, blue and dark blue amid strokes of flame colour or bright green, as in certain sketches by Seurat.

Teams of men and women, in about equal numbers of each sex and dressed in blue, were repairing sections of the road. We came to a large central agricultural store with a market spilling out over the road which narrowed here in order to pass through the village. There was only one line of traffic in each direction, causing a traffic block which seemed irresolvable, especially since traffic going in our direction had spread right over both sides of the road so that at some point further down the traffic coming in the other direction was held up outside the village. Mr Lin saw in all this a breakdown of discipline all too characteristic of rural China. He suddenly changed from being our guide into some other personality such as commander of a section of a People's Army or a Commune Brigade. He jumped out of the car in which I was riding with him and walked down the village street and outside the village till he came to a T-junction where the blockage seemed to originate. David got out of his car and followed him. He told me afterwards that a traffic policeman was vainly struggling to control the traffic. Mr Lin quickly judged him incompetent, and asserting some higher power of magic which everyone instantly recognized to be his, took control of the situation with what seemed only a few rapid passes of his hands. The traffic instantly disentangled itself and we drove on.

David, Gregory and I in fact welcomed the traffic stoppage because it gave us the opportunity to take photographs and observe what was going on in the street. There were dozens of lorries, many buses, hundreds of bicycles, handcarts and barrows pushed by workers, carts drawn by horses or by donkeys, military trucks, a few tractors and very eccentric looking vehicles with engines hoodless and exposed and clanking. Many of the lorries were empty but others were carrying bottles, cartons, huge wicker baskets, bits of machinery, bricks, drain pipes, vegetables. A good many trucks were filled with agricultural workers. From vehicles, or standing at the side of the road, country people smiled, waved at us, gestured to us to photograph them and were altogether friendly.

On nearly all occasions the tourist visiting China has the feeling that he is looking at people (the masses!) through a pane of glass and that they are looking through it back at him. But this was one of the occasions when the pane of glass seemed to have gone and for a few minutes we were merely looking at one another.

As soon as Mr Lin had jumped into the car in which he and I were travelling and we had, in a few seconds, left the village, the road seemed quite empty and we drove through countryside still lusher. There were oxen, teams of two drawing a rake-like wooden plough through a rice field.

We arrived at Hangchow at 11 a.m. – an hour late – and were told by our local guide that we would be left alone till 2.30. The hotel, which was in rather extensive grounds, spread over two or three separate buildings, one of which contained the dining room.

After lunching early, we took the road outside the entrance to our hotel and soon found ourselves at a place where there was a bridge. From here stone steps with grass growing between the stones led down to a very pretty canal with a path running along the side. Here in this little world of the canal below street level there was to our right, beyond an archway, a cluster of old houses, and beyond that, another bridge. David sat half-way down the stone steps, spread out painting things in front of him, opened a large sketchbook and started a painting of the canal, straight and then curving in front of him, like a sickle lying there, with the old houses at the bend, and ripples of water swirling in concentric circles in the foreground.

No sooner had he taken up his brush and drawn in a few lines than he was surrounded by children who seemed to appear from nowhere: boys and girls between three and twelve years old. The older boys wore trousers of a bottle green-blue colour and white shirts with communist red kerchiefs tied loosely round their necks. One girl wore a flowered jacket and had hair prettily drawn up in a knot over the top of her head, and dropping down in a pony tail behind. Another girl had pale mauve trousers and a pullover with short sleeves and a pink flower embroidered in front. A crush of young men, half-hidden by leaves, looked down over a parapet at the edge of the road above us, at David being gently mobbed by these sweet-tempered children. After a time he gave up the attempt to paint, took out his Polaroid camera, and, to their delight, took photographs of the children, which he distributed among them.

David went back with his painting things to the hotel, while Gregory and I strolled along the canal bank. We came to an archway between two small buildings, one of which had a roof with tiles running in two little ripples like circumflex accents over two bricked-up windows below them. The ends of the beams under the roof were painted white, so roof and eaves formed a waving border in parallel lines, painted inside with white spots which showed mysteriously through shadows. The archway framed a space which was an almost perfect circle through which we saw the path and the canal continuing, luminous, as though through a lens. We went through the arch and to our left above the edge of the canal there were pots and wooden bowls with miniature palm trees in them. I thought of that Chinese way of spacing plants out in gardens, as though each were a separate specimen, like an image on a slide, and I suddenly remembered the artist Tang Mu-li talking in his meticulous English and with his bright eagerness choosing each word as though he were pincering a particular morsel between chopsticks. Two small boys played at hiding behind the archway then darting down like minnows to the canal.

We walked along the path by the canal, and then past the backs of the old houses and we came to the bridge which we had seen earlier from the steps. Standing on the bridge, we looked down at the canal; below us, women leaned over the water washing clothes and also, as Gregory pointed out, cleaning fish. From where we stood, the bowls, with the women's heads bent over them, seemed like haloes.

We crossed the bridge and turned left at the end, walking back along the road to the bridge we had first come to, near the hotel. On our way, from the road, we saw between branches, the old houses with their reflections in the water. We saw now that there were two houses separate from each other and connected by a covered platform with a roof over it which was a continuation of the roofs of the houses. The platform or corridor curved with the bend of the canal. Its shape resembled that of a bow. By the roadside, on a copper-sulphate and orange-and-greenish-coloured, lichen-covered stone we noticed a large bright-green caterpillar.

In the afternoon, we were taken by Mr Lin and our local guide to the West Lake (Sai Wu), an enchanted watery park, with walks along the lake shore where you might wander for days, islets, bridges, temples, pavilions, a palace, a great pagoda, and thousands of willow trees – and many pines – that mixture of nature and artifice, one century and another, past and present – not to mention depredation in various wars and rebellions – and reconstruction for tourists – so bewildering for the foreign visitor to China.

We came to a little pavilion, at the end of a peninsula, with a double roof, the ends of the eaves turned up like dogs' ears and perfectly circular openings cut through each wall framing the lake scene on all four sides. Standing there, we saw that each circle was designed to frame a particular view – a picture: one of the pagoda, far distant; another of the seven-pavilioned bridge. David was fascinated, especially by the oval of sunlight rounded by a very black cut-out sihouette of shadow cast on the floor beneath our feet, a linking motif, he said, bringing together the circular openings and the far scenes they looked onto. He said that the effect of a circle or oval, bringing images together and giving diversity unity, was what he had tried to achieve in the Stravinsky sets. Later, when I saw them in New York, I realized that he had done just this.

We then went to see in close-up the seven pavilions perched on their great oblong-stoned impressive bridge.

After the West Lake we went to the lacquer factory. As usual, we were given an introductory talk by a director, about the making of the lacquer, then we looked at specimens arranged in show cases in what was, I suppose, the boardroom: screens, tables, chairs, chests of drawers, picture frames and pictures all lacquer, massive vermilion vases with chrysanthemums carved on their sides, and so on. There was a large panel depicting our old friend the Nanking Bridge in lacquer and a screen of a scholar seated at a table. David admired very much the gradations of colour on the screen: greenish grey of the carpet, Chinese red of the table, and behind the inlay of the figure of the scholar, in the background, shades of dark blue and turquoise.

We were taken over the workshops, long low rooms with many work tables. In the first of these, apprentices – mostly girls, but also a few boys – were chiselling lines, straight or curved, into vermilion lacquer. They followed the design or drawing set beside them on the table at which they were working. In spite of being gaped at, and to some extent pestered, by the troops of us tourists on hourly visits, the apprentices went on cutting hair-thin lines copying the designs before them with the utmost concentration.

David said that his father's job in Bradford (when David was a child) was to draw lines along the metal tubes of bicycle frames. From watching him do this, David learned how to draw a perfectly straight line by holding his thumb at a certain angle and pushing it along the edge of the metal tube, the brush between his fingers. Now he asked one of the apprentices what he did if he made a mistake when cutting a line through a surface which was one of the hundred or so layers of paint from which the lacquer was built up. The boy delighted him by answering that the situation did not arise. No one ever did make a mistake here. David said his father would have made the same reply.

In the next room we entered, they were painting, with the finest of brushes dipped into little pots of gold paint, lines straight – and curved – surrounds for patterns of

Tools for lacquer work

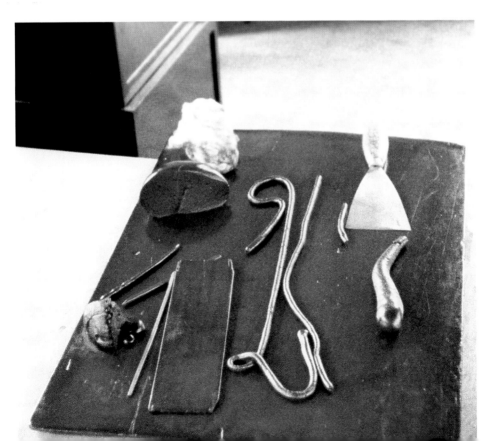

flowers or birds or other animals, or dragons made of mother-of-pearl or semi-precious stones inlaid in the lacquer. These craftsmen had the look of total absorption – beautiful – of highly skilled artists in their separate world of making. One young man was copying freehand with a brush onto the lacquer from a pencilled design in front of him. A girl was painting in five colours from separate pots like petals contained in a circular enamel box.

I think David liked the lacquer factory as much as anything we saw before we visited Canton. The whole place, as we saw, when we went outside into the lanes and yards, was a village industry. There were separate buildings, none of them over three storeys, many of them of only one storey, with triangular roofs and large windows with pathways between each and a road down the centre. David got people to look out of the windows of the main three-storeyed buildings, and photographed the whole façade, with faces peering out of the windows.

In the yards there were notice boards, sometimes with chalk drawings on them. One of a girl seen in profile, weaving, I think, another of a very animated Mickey Mouse-like bicycle, drawn in one continuous thick white line.

In the workshops David photographed the chisels, brushes, scrapers, stilettos – and strange instruments whose names I do not know – of the lacquer workers: the thick glutinous vermilion, turquoise, yellow, saffron, green, brown and black shining enamels – and the gold paint.

Before we left, the director of the factory asked me to write a poem for the factory workers. At first I wanted to say no, this would be unthinkable, but then I thought that to refuse would seem, in their eyes, rudeness, so I agreed. I started thinking about the Chinese attitude (shared by the Japanese) towards painting a picture or writing a poem for a particular occasion. The improvisation, a gesture of pure offering or celebration, is a Chinese and Japanese custom.

Of course, I scarcely slept that night, but towards dawn saw, as I thought, my way to a poem, which referred to their art, their skill and praised them as the heirs of their ancient craft.

My idea came from our walk along the shores of the West Lake, where we greatly admired the bridge that had seven pavilions on it. With their uptilted peaked roofs, they looked like the wings and tail feathers of birds sitting on a stone pediment, the arches of the bridge. My idea was that I should pay the lacquer craftsmen the compliment of saying that if the Seven Pavilioned bridge asked them to reproduce its image in lacquer on a screen (I was thinking of the panel depicting the modern bridge done in lacquer) they would do so with skill equalling that of the eighteenth-century craftsmen who had built the bridge. I wrote the poem on the assumption that the buildings in the parks of the West Lake are eighteenth century, but on reading Nagel's Guide after my return to London I find no reference to the seven-pavilioned bridge, and a chilling paragraph in the section discussing 'The Western

Chalk drawing of girl weaving

Side of the Lake' begins, 'The present buildings are all recent. The Temple was destroyed during the Taiping rebellion, and was not rebuilt before the early 20th century.' An occupational risk of a visitor to China is to discover that the temple he has been admiring has been destroyed and he is only looking at a modern replacement. He may even, I gather, be taken to a museum which, with all its contents, is an exact replica of another museum, the first museum being so crowded that the authorities decided it would be a good idea to have a second.

The Chinese during their risings seem, in common with other nations, addicted to destroying their ancient monuments, some of the worst such depredations being quite recent, having occurred during the Cultural Revolution. Well, I had better own up to the poem.

Here it is:

WITH THANKS TO THE CRAFTSMEN OF HANGCHOW WHO SHOWED US THEIR
LACQUER FACTORY

If the seven-pavilioned bridge of the Lesser Western Lake
Should beg to have itself transferred to lacquer
You would grant its wish, o craftsmen of Hangchow,
With skill no less than that those craftsmen showed
Who built it here two hundred years ago.

31 May

Mr Lin, when I handed the poem over to him after my sleepless night, seemed pleased and took great pains with the translation (I wish the poem had been worthier of his trouble). While he walked in the grounds of the Buddhist temple the next morning, he held a piece of paper in front of him and wrote, and scratched out, and wrote again and again, just as I did when writing the original. I had subjected him to some of the agony I myself underwent. I was grateful that he tried to make it exact because the poem has no merit apart from the attempt to say something, even if what it said was wrong.

When we went to the Hangchow art school after luncheon, we had further evidence of the Chinese pleasure in the art of improvising. The director, a round-faced genial host, received us with the usual formalities. As we sat facing him drinking tea, he told us about the art school and how it had fared under the Gang of Four. Later we went to his office-cum-studio which was pleasantly informal. A kind of laundry line onto which letters, bills and more drawings were pegged ran from the window to a table. A desk was littered with rolled up or unrolled sheets of paper on which students had made brush marks representing leaves, flowers, birds.

The director, serene and smiling, with a gently welcoming expression on his face, walked over to the table, took up a sheet of paper, flattened it and, turning courteously to David, asked: 'What subject would you like?' David, who had been study-

*The director of
the art school*

ing paintings and drawings which were stuck on the walls, said: 'Leaves.' (Earlier, he had looked at a painting of leaves which he knew to be by the director and remarked to me that it showed real observation.) The director nodded, looked down intently at the sheet of paper, with a silent movement of his lips almost like praying (I remembered how in Delhi I had seen Indian musicians bow their heads in prayer before taking up their instrument). Then he took a brush, dipped it in a flask of water and after that into some black colour in a saucer in front of him on the table. Then with what musicians call 'attack' he pressed the loaded brush against the paper. He made a large wet blot which he then worked across with rapid brush strokes, occasionally lifting his brush to add – on a different part of the paper – more blots in the shape of leaves. Then he painted into the still wet leaf-shapes the lines of veins. He looked appraisingly at the marks he had made, and next, attacking again, with a few brisk strokes from the tip of the brush he drew in twigs connecting the leaves to the branch. Later, he chose a purplish colour and

splashed in some grapes. Then, with the tip of his brush and using black again, he connected the grapes to tendrils.

The painting was finished, he handed it to David who looked at it with interest and thanked him. The director now took up a second sheet of paper and asked me what I would like painted. Without pausing to reflect, I said, 'a grass-hopper' (I love grass-hoppers). He hesitated a moment and then asked, would I mind having a fish? I said I would be delighted. The same gesture, the same poised brush and then attack, and in a quarter of an hour he had produced two goggle-eyed goldfish swimming in water that was the paper, while, under this surface, flat horizontal lines were the leaves of water lilies floating on the surface.

All this happened while half a dozen students who had filed into the studio (they had not been there during our formal introductions) stood around watching

with the shining eyes and half-open lips of young people watching the ballet, the dance of brush on paper. (It was difficult to associate them with rowdies of their age of the Cultural Revolution, little more than ten years ago.)

David said he had never used Chinese brushes and paints before and that he would like to try them out. Paper, brushes and paints were brought. Asked what subject he intended to paint, David said he would do a portrait of the director. The director promptly seated himself at the end of the table and kept prodigiously still, with a faint alluring smile on his face. David made a few inquiries about the materials that were set before him. He dipped his brush first in the water and then in the saucer of black paint and began to draw lines across the paper. He used the brush as a pointed pencilling instrument, not as the impress of different stylized marks on the paper, in the Chinese manner. His attention was divided equally between his looking at the expanse of the director's face and his drawing in progress on the paper. The difference between the Eastern and the Western approach seemed demonstrable. The traditionalist Chinese artist draws upon a repertory of themes which he interprets with instruments, which are brushes, as stylized in their phrasing as a violin or a flute playing traditional music. The Western artist looks at the model as much as at the picture he is making and subdues his instrument –

the brush – for the purpose of making it realize the image. I do not mean by this that he does not pay attention to the character of the pigment or that he is unaware of brushwork, but the first object of his attention is usually the image, even if this is abstract (except for *tachiste* painting.)

The difference between Eastern and Western approaches was here demonstrated in an exaggerated, over-simple way. For, on the one hand, the Hangchow painters were completely traditionalist, unaware, it seemed, of the existence of modernism, and, on the other, David was painting with Chinese materials for the first time. Moreover he had chosen to do a portrait, drawing from the model, and not to improvise from his imagination. Later that day David bought Chinese brushes and paints and then proceeded to write postcards to his friends in imitation Chinese calligraphy.

The director seemed pleased with David's portrait of him. He took sheets of paper again and spread them out on the table weighing the corners down with stones. Taking up his brush, this time he wrote inscriptions in calligraphy, one for David, one for me and one for Mr Lin. The words celebrated our visit as a sign of friendship 'between our two countries'. I found the reminder that our visit was a public event in the history of both our nations chilling. I don't like being thought of as a nation.

Our next visit was to a jade factory – modernized only to the extent that the students carved jade with electric tools – making one think, as one entered their workshop, of an army of dentists seated working at benches.

Once again a master of ceremonies, the director, told us that Hangchow was the cradle of jade work which had begun here during the T'ang dynasty. Many of the great treasures shown in Peking were made here. David asked whether the factory had been closed during the Cultural Revolution, and the director said, yes. He went on to say that all over the world the rich cling to masterpieces of jade as they would to diamonds. Unlike many other things, the longer you cling to objects of jade carved by fine craftsmen, the more valuable they get.

What he was saying is, of course, true, though I am not sure of the value the rich attach to jade carved by communist craftsmen. But the strange contradiction implicit in what he was saying struck me. The function of the rich as sustainer of values was being recognized here in China where anyone rich enough to buy the perfectly plain jade bowl which I longed for and which was quite beyond my means would be regarded as a class enemy, if not a criminal. Yet by implication the director was also admitting that the rich buy jade objects because they are amateurs of the rare and beautiful, whereas no one in China is able to possess rare and beautiful things. It is the government that buys and only for two reasons: firstly in order to sell abroad; secondly, to put jade objects in some museum. Thus the things that in capitalist countries individuals choose because they are valuable, in socialist countries committees choose for the masses to look at in museums, or to sell to the capitalist. Of course, as long as they continue to make *objets de valeur* identical with those made in the past, it is reasonable that the market for them consists of members

of the class which has been overthrown by the revolution. But to say this is to arouse misgivings. Although the objects may look exactly the same as they did in the old days, is it not possible that in some way – perhaps scarcely discernible – they lack conviction? Moreover, how is it that they cannot produce objects in jade which express the conviction of the socialist society? Little statues in jade of Karl Marx or Mao Tse-tung, or Chou En-lai, for example? Abstractions of Marxist-Leninist-Maoist thought?

An art school of three hundred students was attached to the jade factory, in a separate building. I went there after looking at jade objects which were offered on sale to tourists at the end of the visit to the factory – I bought bracelets for my grand-daughters – and found David seated in the middle of a great crowd of students, doing an academic art school drawing of an Italianate, almost Art Nouveau bust of a lady whose shoulders were swathed in what was evidently an evening dress made of, perhaps, velvet. She had an Edwardian hair-do, rather difficult to draw, I should think, and David said he was not finding his task easy, he had not drawn from such a model for over thirty years. The bust was illuminated on both sides, by two naked electric light bulbs.

1 June

In the morning we returned briefly to the art school to photograph the director, together with his students, outside the building. David had brought his Polaroid camera. The students were delighted, laughing, crowding round us, fascinated by the whirr with which the Polaroid emits its little piece of shiny white paper which, within a few seconds, turns yellow and then, chameleon-like, changes to reveal all the colours of objects it was exposed to – in this case more than twenty grinning students – under their smiling eyes.

Next, we were taken to a Buddhist temple – the Ling Yin Si – in a beautiful setting of rocky hills and ancient trees. Although going back to the early fourth century, when the temple was founded by a holy man from India who claimed to recognize in the hill where it stands, as Nagel's Guide puts it, 'a corner of Mount Grdhrakuta "which had flown there", . . . the present buildings are all recent'. Much damage was done to these holy places during the Taiping rebellion in 1853, when Hangchow was the capital of the revolution.

I comfort myself that so good is the art of restoring monuments in China that only the expert can really distinguish between the original temples and those that have been restored. The temple and its garden are beautiful. We walked up steps into a portico which contains statues of four giants, stridently coloured and fantastically arrayed. In their gaudy extravagance they reminded me of statues in rococo churches in Bavarian villages which seem peasant versions of princely art. These four giants are the four generals in charge of the four gates of heaven. Accoutred with every sign of power, they are out of some childish nightmare. They lack dignity and nobility and seem to yell 'fee fi fo fum' to all comers while shaking their sceptres, wobbling their crowns, clanking with cannibalistic laughter.

At the centre of the entrance hall, back to back, there are two golden Buddhas with bronze urns in front of them. The one in front is a genial host who welcomes you inside. The other, back to back with him, is a severe guardian frowning, and resolved to keep you out if your are an evil spirit. Having passed these figures, we crossed a stone courtyard and went into another hall, still a place of worship. Two priests were there, one old, the other almost posthumous, his skull seeming to press through his parchment skin – death yearning to be a new-born baby. I took them to be the last monks of China but later I noticed two scraggy emaciated boys with shorn heads and sallow skin holding tapers before an altar.

In this hall there were eighteen golden Buddhas placed in front of three other, very tall ones, in accordance with some hierarchy among Buddhas: Buddha one to eighteen. These Buddhas had facial expressions illustrative of diverse emotions, the whole series from one to eighteen reminding me of those ancient books on the Art of Drawing which show varieties of passion in physiognomy with lips curled back and eyes narrowed and with wrinkles round them to express delight, teeth bared and forehead frowning to signify contempt, etc.

Beyond this hall, in a corridor so narrow that we had to stand very close to the wall behind us to view on the opposite side a painting of a waterfall symbolizing divinity cascading a cornucopia of goodies – a Father Christmas stocking of presents with scenes of nature promising paradise painted into it. David said:

See how the architecture obliges you to stand up close in order to see it and be overwhelmed.' He said he was inspired with new ideas for opera sets through having seen this painting.

We went outside into a further courtyard where a path led to a wall with one of those slotted openings, like shining lenses, which are such a feature of Chinese gardens. Through it we could see a rock garden and hills, and, beyond, a temple. Going through this entrance we came to a steeply descending path leading to an archway of great stone slabs heaped, as it seemed, almost haphazardly on one another, as though one of the giant Buddhist generals had taken to stone masonry for a hobby. Beyond this we came to a garden of large stones of irregular size and ragged rocks bored through with holes – those rocks that make me think of early Romantic garden architecture, like Alexander Pope's grotto.

It was a garden of rocks, all at different levels, and with, high up, a pavilion in the midst. On top of each rock stood an Overseas Chinese tourist, being photographed. The scene was strange, at once hilarious and a bit awesome, like the roof of a gothic cathedral with spires, on each the statue of a saint.

Finally, we came to a little lake at one end of which there was a shelter where souvenirs were sold. In front of it, there was a platform, with a railing at the edge, where many people were crowding, looking down into the chalk-blue water at two shoals of goldfish which were rotating like catherine wheels, side by side, and, just above the level of the water, a terracotta pot with a lotus in it, flowering pink and with green leaves between them.

In the afternoon we left Hangchow by car, and then continued by train to our next destination, Wusih.

On our way to catch the train, we had to cross the Yangtze by a car ferry, proceeding from one flat characterless shore across the even flatter muddy river – with a few of those wonderful quilted sails on it that seem to have floated into today out of a remote piratical trading past – to an equally flat characterless shore on the further side.

Chinese railway compartments are divided into two classes, 'hard' and 'soft'. Tourists, of course, travel 'soft'. The compartment was extremely comfortable, a home from hotel with, between the seats, tables with lace tablecloths on which were placed pots of flowers. David was delighted. We found ourselves in a compartment with a group of Chinese from Singapore, smartly dressed, pampered, carrying cameras – blatantly everything that the Chinese of the People's Republic are not. One marvels at the extraordinary chameleon-like qualities of the Chinese in acquiring the coloration of different backgrounds into which they are fitted. The Hong Kong Chinese seem utterly different from those of mainland China; those of San Francisco, London and France, all different. Where are the Chinese really Chinese? I assume, of course, that the answer is mainland China. But within China itself they change – the most obvious difference being between townsman and peasant. And everyone remarks that the populace, the masses, are utterly different

Table and flowers for 'soft'-class travellers

from what they were before the Liberation. I cannot believe, however, that these regimented millions are the final manifestation. I assume, again, that the revolution liberated in them their true Chinese character. We noticed that in China itself the people seemed much happier, and perhaps therefore truer to their innate character, when they were free to trade, as large sections of the population now are. Surely, the Chinese like being small traders. Under their drab uniforms they seem individualists.

Wusih (Wuxi)

When we got to Wusih we were met by two cars and a local guide, Mr Wang Po-shen. We were driven through a characterless modern main street, and then suddenly came to a square of two-storey buildings which looked like a section of some medieval city in the European lowlands – Ghent or Bruges perhaps. The cars did not stop and we were so startled by this vision that we did not ask the drivers to stop and let us take photographs. Perhaps it was a dream, for I have been unable to find any description in the Guide Book corresponding to what we thought we saw as we passed through.

The hotel, ten storeys high, and built of concrete, seemed to aspire to be the Wusih-Hilton. Downstairs there were notices advertising disco and dancing going on till midnight. The dining room resembled a cavernous dance hall or a movie theatre, empty looking despite the white tablecloths and the many guests, under a great ceiling with white panels in diamond patterns. On one wall there was a huge Chinese landscape, a lifeless example of the traditional style carried out at the academy. The food was the least tasty of any we had in China.

Wusih buildings: ancient and modern

2 June

After breakfast we were taken on a tour of the canal at Wusih on a smart motor launch which quickly filled up with expensive-looking American tourists. Most of the women were wearing shirts and trousers in mauves and yellows, shocking pinks and shining greens, perfectly laundered. The men, in check, or flowered, or plain-coloured shirts and plaid or russet trousers, had lined, distinguished faces with skin looking drip-dried. Some women appeared bored as people going abroad not to be bored, but finding themselves in exactly the same set as they left behind in Florida or California.

Canal-side scenes These boat trips through Wusih take place, I suppose, daily, and for the Chinese 'masses' who stand in the roadway, or on the canal bank, or in backyards, or on steps leading down to the water, watching us flash by, we must have seemed some kind of showboat lacking only guitars, banjos and song to entertain them. We were for most of the trip near enough to the canal bank for people to smile and wave at us. I cannot believe that they could envy us any more than I can envy spacemen, for we belonged to a world remote from theirs. Few of them could have imagined any circumstances in which they could be propelled into our world. The pleasure the Chinese get from seeing tourists cannot be in the category of what David called vicarious pleasure, which is a mild self-identification. What was real for them, as for us, was the gulf dividing us – the comedy of the fact that the same humanity living at the same time on the same planet really has so little in common. Our boat was like a cage full of gaudy tropical birds. The spectator stares at the plumage, hears the squawks but sees only the gap which divides different stages of evolution. Did they or we here represent the higher form?

During the first few minutes of our trip the boat moved parallel with the road-side, from which we had embarked. We watched the traffic moving behind spaced-out trees at the roadside, and behind the bicycles and vehicles were shops. People stood at the edge of the road staring at our launch and at the other canal traffic. Later the canal diverged from the road, so that the view became blocked out by houses. Now what we saw was no longer traffic, but, in yards and on paths, separate scenes: a cabinet-maker working at the construction of what looked like a hen-coop, placed upside down on a table, standing in a yard; an old woman, half-frowning, half-smiling as we went by, standing beside a white-and-yellow earthenware jar

high as her waist; four dungareed workers holding jugs in their hands, standing smiling before piled-up white stone blocks. On each side of us houses fronted the canal. Most of them had white-plaster walls. The lines of tiles on their roofs sloped down diagonally towards us, somehow resembling poles covered with cork bark.

Sometimes there were stone-flagged quaysides between houses and steps leading down to the canal at the bottom of which women stooped, washing linen in the dense-looking water. In one such group I noticed a woman wearing a red jacket with approximately matching red shoes. She contrasted with her companions in their blue or bottle-green uniform clothes. Some washerwomen put down their things and stood up very straight to watch us as we sped past. Exceptionally there was a young man stripped of his shirt who was rubbing water onto the white hairless skin of his chest, apart from the others. Shirts blown out by the wind and streaming from cords connected at each end to crossed bamboo staves were blown by the wind to shapes of kites or balloons, even calligraphy. We passed a building yard where men stood among oblong piles of bricks which they heaped up while others unloaded bricks from the hold of a barge. The bricks were vermilion. Further along men were building a wall. We passed women wearing gauze masks over mouths and nostrils. They had colds and were obeying rules to avoid spreading infection. On all sides children, separately or in twos or threes, jumped up, standing looking at us with brilliant shining smiles. Many waved. Our launch went under a bridge which had a stone balustrade against which people leaned resting their elbows as they looked down watching the river traffic and our flamboyant showboat. From below we saw the balustrade above us crowded with faces,

limbs, handles and wheels of bicycles. And looking ahead of us, the bridge framed the vista of irregular forms of houses each side of the canal, with boats on the water and a further bridge. Red flags made splashes of vermilion between water and sky like distributed touches of this primary colour in Renaissance paintings. Further on we came to a quayside area with trucks and packing cases on wharfs, and, in the background, tall derricks and cranes. After this the canal splayed out into the estuary. As we left the shore behind, life on the estuary took on a different noisy activity. There were hundreds of craft of the most varied kinds hooting, jostling one another, thrusting on the eye and deafening to the ear. This trip seemed a marine version of the traffic on the roads out of Peking. It gave the same sense of impetus, of clattering machinery surging forward. It also provided us with a succession of vignettes of this life, on roads, along the canal's edge and on the road that was the canal itself. There were boats with chugging motors and cabins like huts, with little gaps or windows in them through which the barge men – or, sometimes, the barge women – peered. A youth leaned forward pressing his whole body against the shaft of a sweeping oar that was as long as the boat itself; another stood at the stern of the boat, steering it with extended oar.

At last the estuary merged into the open sea. The traffic gathered speed, its noises becoming more and more intermittent, dispersed on the air, houses on the shore became warehouses, tall, huge and broad, there were wharves and factories, larger ships, and barges strung together.

After being returned to the roadside quay from which we had set off, we were shepherded to the main touristic store in Wusih, where we bought only rolls of film. From there we were hurried to the headquarters of the Travel Bureau. We were given beer in a garden just off the street. The local guide produced his local information. At Wusih, he told us, there are factories for making Diesel engines, TV sets, watches, electronic goods and, with Japanese aid, machine tools.

For some reason the conversation got onto the subject of population. The guide said, with a slight edge to his voice, which we seemed to note when our instructors gave way to an impulse to step out of the official role, that in China it was compulsory for families to have not more than one child. Mr Lin took exception to the word 'compulsory' with a glance that seemed to say 'tut tut'. I asked the guide how the government could possibly compel this limitation. Mr Lin answered. He said they couldn't compel it, especially not in the northern part of the country, in the countryside. Persuasion was possible, however: 'by a whole series of measures', interrupted our guide. 'For instance, you get progressively less family assistance for the upbringing of each additional child after the first, less aid in education. Benefits are withdrawn.'

David put in that he wasn't sure what he felt about abortion, but he was certain that if you tried to restrict every family to having only one child, you created as many new problems as you solved. 'What would a whole nation of only children be like?', he asked, and added, 'Why, I am one of a family of four. What would I have been like if I were an only child without brothers and sisters?' I said, 'Yes, I happen

SS with Wang Po-shen

to be one of a family of four also, but the prospect for China if the birth rate is not controlled is that of having a population double the size of its present one of 1,000,000,000. Already a population of 1,200,000,000 is projected for the year 2000. Doubling the present figure would mean that all the social advances made by China in raising the standard of living, and in health, would be swallowed up in Malthusian fashion by the increase of the population. The Chinese would soon become like the Indians.'

David went on being indignant at the idea of one family, one child. I understood his feelings but remained convinced that, apart from nuclear war, the greatest danger to the world in the foreseeable future is over-population. I could not but feel that the best contribution China is making today for the general good of humanity is in the attempt to control population growth. Though it seems just like the Chinese, I thought, to put things in this sloganish-statistical way. They are always thinking in terms of multiples of units: the 200,000 workmen who built the Imperial Palace between 1407 and 1420, the 700,000 volunteers who built the mausoleum for Mao Tse-tung between October 1976 and August 1977, the Four Modernizations, and so on. David argued against the view that science, in this case the Pill, should facilitate policies which he regarded as inhuman. Human behaviour should not, he thought, be submitted to scientific necessity. On the contrary, science was there to help provide feasible solutions to human needs. He didn't believe over-population was the overwhelming problem sociologists and other experts presented it as being. I didn't agree, but I saw that I accepted too easily as truth the scientific arguments and that in accepting scientific arguments one may be jettisoning the insight of the imagination into human nature.

We left the little garden where we had been arguing and were taken to the upper room of a restaurant where we were entertained by the director of the Travel Bureau. He was a courteous, distinguished looking man, dressed in a serge suit and having the look of an intelligent army officer. He was polite and hospitable, entertaining and not just lecturing us when he made his introductory remarks.

He said – and our local guide translated: 'In Wusih there is a tradition of eating local dishes on festive occasions. The cuisine is sweetish and comes for the most part from exploiting the resources of lake and land in the neighbourhood, using these materials fresh and with very little fat and cooking them well enough for them to be easy to digest. No frozen fish is put into the dishes we are about to eat. Chickens exercise freely and are fed partly on snails, which makes their flavour more delectable. There are several kinds of fish in the lake,' he went on, 'and we will sample a few of them. The most eminent of these is called the Mandarin fish, given that name because it feeds on shrimps and less significant fry. It is also called cassia.' David interrupted here to ask whether the Mandarin fish had always been known by that name, or had been given it since the Liberation. 'Always', was the reply.

We were served with hors d'oeuvre consisting of shrimp, roast duck and several meats, all of them cold. After that, of the dishes I remember – the constituents of one dish were duck's tongues and fried clams; another dish was fried eels – straight from the lake (we saw one such eel when we went on the lake later that afternoon). Finally, there came a dish in which there was some kind of pancake that crackled like fireworks when dipped into a bowl of hot sauce. Our host smiled and said: 'We judge a dish by taste, colour, the order in which the courses are served, and – one last thing – by sound. That we call the Taste of Heaven.' It was a relief, in puritanical China, to have a glimpse of a country in which people still enjoyed cakes and ale.

Wusih, our host said, has a history of 3,200 years. It was called just 'Wush', which means tin, a little over 2,000 years ago when the ore was first discovered here. Then, when the mine became exhausted the name was changed to 'Wusih', meaning 'without tin'. The hill where the mine once was still exists. In the present century, Wusih has, since 1914, become a centre of the textile industry. This is still important, and the city exports silk (just), cotton wool and synthetic fibre.

Our local guide, Mr Wang, told us that he had travelled with a group of Chinese to Greenville, North Carolina, and also to Italy (Milan). I asked him whether they had made these journeys in order to export goods from Wusih. 'No,' he said, but to buy machinery for blending silk and polyester fibres. David said that he hated polyester. The guide laughed and said: 'I hate half our product, too.'

I asked our host what plans there were for the future of Wusih. He said that Wusih would become still more industrialized. 'Would not this spoil it for tourism?' I asked. He replied that the industrial area would be kept separate from the 'scenic'.

David asked what they intended to do about the old architecture: the houses along the canal, the medieval-looking square. Our guide said: 'We aren't going to pull those down. To do so would be vandalism. We will keep all that.'

I asked what the procedure was, when they made plans, for putting them into effect. They said the plans were drawn up by the local congress of the people of Wusih. These had to be sent to Peking for approval. They said that if the plan was not carried out well, officials would be subject to criticism by the congress.

I asked how this local congress was elected. The guide said that, as a matter of fact, there was an election taking place just now. All citizens over 18 years old could vote. To begin with, anyone could nominate whomever he liked: 'for instance,' he said, 'if you were Chinese and a native of Wusih, I could nominate you. Then a list is drawn up of those nominees who receive the most votes.' David asked whether the nominees had to be Party members. The answer was, by no means. For the Party Congress, of course, all the members had to belong to the Party, but not for the local elections.

David said that in England he had never in his life voted in a local election (neither have I). He thought that in local elections in England candidates pretended to be following the policy of their political party, but actually they were often participating in local feuds or serving local interests of which he neither knew nor cared about in the least. I said I felt the same way but that England was such a small country that local issues tended to become microscopic (whether the traffic went up the street one way or the other, put in David): but here they were voting on such questions as to what extent a whole province of China should be industrialized, and where the industries should be located.

What is clear is that the local electors vote in accordance with their own views as to the qualities of local candidates and their attitudes to particular problems. There is no choice as between political parties, since the only party allowed is the Communist Party.

After lunch we were taken on a trip in a tourist motor launch on Lake Tai. The surroundings were very beautiful, with the clean curves of the hills and wooded headlands. At one point there was a pavilion with a gold roof resting on its six columns through which you could see the boughs of pine trees and the water beyond. There were junks with their seamed sails like sumptuous quilted counterpanes, sampans with their masts laid back like the long feathery antennae of some nocturnal moth. We stopped at a place where there was a neck of land and climbed up a hillside along a path that zigzagged among rocks to a tea house. To reach our next stop we had to climb through a park whose main feature was a magnificent example of the ragged rocks fished up from the bottom of this very lake. These rocks do not lose their fascination for me. The Chinese like them so much because they regard them, not, I suppose, as Surrealist objects or prototypes for early Henry Moore sculptures with holes through them (which is how I tend to think of them), but as features of garden architecture, rockeries. Rocks are considered beautiful in themselves. From this path there were views of the lake and of the shore opposite, seen through inverted commas of willow branches and their leaves. We went to another Buddhist temple, flame-coloured and with a little kiosk of a twin-roofed pavilion like a foot-stool in front of it.

I thought about the upturned roofs of pavilions and temples, that the larger ones were like gently upward curving pine boughs, petrified, their tiles like scales taken from the pine-cones: some perky pavilions and kiosks suggested a flirtation of fan-tail pigeons, with tails uplifted, necks intertwined.

The temple had the same arrangement inside as the Buddhist temple we had seen the previous day, with a portico containing four gigantic threatening yet comical generals (rather like Khrushchev banging a shoe on a desk), garishly painted, and incorporating in their clothes legendary attributes and geographical features absorbed into them like rivers into the prose of *Finnegans Wake*.

On our way down from the temple I mentioned to the young man who was our guide that I was always impressed by the peacefulness of Buddhist temples. He said, yes, they were very peaceful. Then he went on to say that for health reasons, both physical and mental, he went in for Buddhist exercises. 'What do you do?' I asked, interested. 'I contemplate for half an hour every day, if I can manage it.' 'How do you contemplate?' 'I sit very still and try to empty my mind of every thought and distraction.' 'Then what happens . . .?' 'It slows down the breathing and metabolism.' 'And do you have the experience of thinking as a vacuous activity without your being aware of actually thinking of anything?' 'Not entirely. Thoughts do come into my mind.' 'What, for example?' 'For example, what can I do most to help a poet and a painter who have come from England to visit me.' I think: what a nice young man, and look down at my wobbly knees and big feet. He goes on, 'Of course, this has nothing to do with religion.' 'There is no spiritual aspect of it?' 'No, it is entirely physiological.' For some reason, my attitude to him changes completely. Materialism. Science, in its help-yourself form. I start thinking of those books which sell better than almost any others today in America about how best to fulfil your potentialities. I remember how in Japan the bestseller of all time is Samuel Smiles's *Self-Help*. The Orient can change so easily from the mysterious to the vapid.

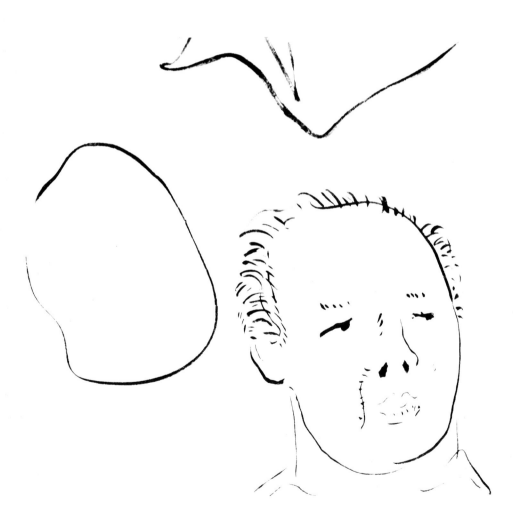

3 June

This morning we went to two silk spinning and weaving factories and also, later on, to a silkworm farm. The first factory was occupied with the process of unwinding the silk from the chrysalis, enwound, to quote Yeats, 'like Hades' bobbin bound in mummy-cloth'. The second factory was for weaving it into cloth.

As a boy I used to keep silkworms (to judge from the imagery in Yeats's 'Byzantium', I suspect that he did too). They were obtained from a naturalist's shop near the British Museum. I kept them in a box with sides made of perforated zinc. When a chrysalis was formed I used to put it into a bowl of hot water and then pull the end of thread till all the silk was unwound onto a card. I was pleased to discover that the silkworm chrysalises of Wusih are robbed of their precious silk in much the same way – though before the process of unwinding they are put into a huge cauldron and boiled so that the pupae inside the chrysalises are killed.

Before the silk is removed, the chrysalises are graded A, B and C. The grading is done by girls seated alongside a running band on which the chrysalises are placed. The girls sort them out, throwing away discoloured or rotted ones, and distributing them into A, B or C baskets. Together with some American tourists, we watched the girls doing this. Two of the American ladies fished a reject out of a rubbish bin and, holding it up in front of a girl sorter, one of them instructed their guide: 'Please ask her why this cocoon has been thrown out. It seems perfectly healthy to us.' The guide inquired of the girl and then reported back: 'She says two caterpillars got together and have woven their chrysalis into one cocoon, so this chrysalis not healthy' – an example I suppose, of Chinese puritanism applied to the animal kingdom.

If seeing girls having to keep up with the chrysalises jogging on the running band made one a bit concerned, what we saw on the next floor was like some description of a factory in early nineteenth-century New England by Herman Melville. The girls were busy unwinding the thread from the already graded chrysalises, by machine. A row of them fed bobbins with thread from cocoons floating in water in front of them. When a cocoon had been exhausted of its thread, the girl in whose tray it was had to throw it out of the water and connect another cocoon to a bobbin on the machine above her. As each girl had to supply her machine with about twenty threads running into bobbins, and the cocoons became rapidly depleted of their thread, this process required each girl's total attention. They sat there in a row in front of the vertical threads leading out of the water trays, constantly having to dart out their hands to throw away a depleted cocoon or connect up the thread of a new one to the spool. They looked like a row of frenetic jazz pianists.

I thought that from the point of view of such a worker, it cannot really matter very greatly whether she is working in a communist or a capitalist country – except that, given the differences in living standards and stages of historical development, she would today be better off in the capitalist country. Communism was here, as David pointed out, undergoing what corresponded to the early stages of capitalist development. And the girls were better off than they would have been under

nineteenth-century capitalism. Admittedly, I have never seen a silk factory in a capitalist society. As often happens with tourists when visiting foreign countries, they see there conditions of which they would never see the corresponding ones in their own country.

We went next to the factory where the silk was woven into fabrics. This was very much as we expected: looms automatically weaving cloth with patterns on instruction cards coded by the artist-designers. We were taken to the sales room and shown lengths of silk with the patterns woven into them. I thought I would choose dress lengths of silk for my wife and daughter. David teased me: 'All you can do is just stand there staring at these patterns in a daze. You know you're completely incapable of choosing one rather than another.' But when I asked him to help me choose, he admitted that from the point of view of us Western would-be importers of Chinese silks, there were, by American or European standards, simply no patterns worth choosing – in striking contrast to Japan or North Korea where one can find beautiful designs, by our standards. The Chinese silks we saw corresponded to David's judgment pronounced when looking at the shop windows of Sian – French provincial of the 1930s. The patterns were, most of them, traditional chinoiserie, but less good than those woven in the days when these fabrics were hand-made.

What we felt about the silks we felt even more strongly about work produced at the clay figurine and doll factory which we were taken to see in the afternoon. Comparing the modern products with the old ones, of characters in traditional theatre and opera which are preserved there in showcases, is to feel embarrassed at the worse-than-Disneyland vulgarity of what is produced today.

After visiting the silk factories we went to a silkworm farm in the countryside. In the fields, not far from the road, there was a conglomeration of houses. Of these, the main one had a façade consisting of a wall upcurving against the sky like a ship's side and prow. Mr Lin told me that these old houses were built like stylized ships as a protection against ill-fortune. This had formerly been the house of a squire of the neighbourhood. It was now part of a farm. The other houses were really extensions and barns or sheds built up against or alongside the gray lichenous façade. Between a row of trees and the façade there was an orange-coloured sandy path, very beautiful against the wall's grey-blues in reflected lights from shimmering leaves.

Here one was in the special world peculiar to old farms. Hens were running around and squawking in the yard everywhere, ducks swimming through a miniature canal not more than two feed wide; we noticed, too, that there were stooks of corn heaped up against the wall of a shed. Children played. The silkworms were kept in a large shed: they munched and crunched leaves which were spread out on long shelves or trays. They ate as though eating was an industry. From time to time a girl would pick some of the caterpillars off a tray and throw them onto the ground in another part of the shed, among stubble. With a rotating, swaying movement of the upper half of their bodies they wound the threads of silk around the chrysalis which each was in the process of becoming. It made me imagine a lot of old ladies weaving and winding grave cloths round their plump corpses. At the entrance of this shed, most of the inhabitants of the farm, especially the children, gathered round us and had Polaroid photographs taken of them by David. One small boy was carrying, attached by string to the top of a stick, a large beetle or cockroach, of which he had made a plaything. 'Look,' said David, 'he doesn't have any toys, so he takes a cockroach as a toy for himself.' Mr Lin, always fond of children, carried a small girl in his arms.

We noticed a heap of dried-up mulberry leaves on a shelf. We were told they were full of silkworm shit and that whoever slept on them as a pillow would find a perfect cure for insomnia.

From Wusih we continued to our next destination, Shanghai, by train. On the train Mr Lin got talking about the Cultural Revolution. He said that in Peking it was run by four students from the University. They conducted diatribes against one another. They were also in contact with the Gang of Four who pulled strings, of which they were the dangling puppets, behind the scenes.

He said the phrase the 'Gang of Four' originated with Chairman Mao who, though first encouraging the Cultural Revolution, later warned his wife and her three coadjutors: 'You must not organize yourselves into a Gang of Four.' On the subject of Mao, Mr Lin added that he was one of the best classical scholars in China, that he wrote the best calligraphy of anyone in 700 years, and that he was an excellent poet. He also said that even at the height of his power Chairman Mao never had a salary of more than $500 a month. It struck me that this was a little like saying the Queen of England never had money to go shopping in a London department store.

He said that during the Cultural Revolution the students quoted for their own purposes a saying of Chairman Mao: 'The State is ours. Affairs of the State should be in our hands. If we don't take care of things, who else will?'

He told us of statements and ideas put forward by the students in the Cultural Revolution. These remind me of Surrealist ideas in Auden's *The Orators*: all postmen should wear red uniforms; the police should direct traffic waving not batons, but copies of Chairman Mao's *Little Red Book*; no pictures of Chairman Mao should be exhibited which did not show both his ears; traffic lights should be altered so that *green* signified STOP and *red* FORWARD; no one should be permitted to put a portrait of Chairman Mao on sale, since representations of him should not be the objects of mercenary transaction. At that time, Mr Lin said, badges depicting Chairman Mao got every day bigger and bigger.

Mr Lin returned to the subject of the conversation he and I had had with Simon in Nanking. I asked him what principles of criticism were permissible in China. He said there were four basic ones: (1) No matter what your criticism you must accept the principles of Marxist-Leninist-Maoist thought; (2) you must accept the necessity (irreversibility) of the dictatorship of the proletariat; (3) you must respect the Party leadership; (4) within these limits you are free to criticize.

On another occasion, I asked him whether he believed that the state would at some time wither away. 'Oh yes,' he said, 'I do most certainly believe that.' 'Well, when do you think it will happen?' I asked. 'In a thousand years,' he said, and seeing me look startled, he said: 'Or maybe two thousand.' I looked hard at him. He seemed perfectly serious, and I reflected that the Chinese do take a long view of history. The millennial view of life is where communism is closest to primitive Christianity.

4 June Shanghai

We are staying at the Shanghai Mansions, once a British residential hotel, built in the 1920s. I have an immense airless suite all to myself (the air-conditioning does not function). The rooms seem about twenty feet high. There is a large sitting room with a huge leather sofa and armchairs, writing desk and TV, cupboards that look like gothic cubicles, a bedroom like a stage set, with damask-covered double bed beyond folding doors, a bathroom with a great curved marble wash basin, a huge bath and lots of engraved silver knobs. All it lacks is a great imperial propeller of a fan, suspended from the ceiling. I do wish it had one.

So much of China makes me think of poetry, not just because it is poetic but because it corresponds to descriptions of things in English poetry. My bedroom here recalls a stiflingly over-odorous poem by Robert Browning entitled 'Love in a Lifetime':

> *Heart, fear nothing, for, heart, thou shalt find her –*
> *Next time herself! – not the trouble behind her*
> *Left in the curtain, the couch's perfume!*

One imagines an empire builder, a colonel, tall and with a dark fringe of moustache staying here, and accompanying him his languorous wife, all stuffed into taffeta, overripe.

> *As she touched it, the cornice-wreath blossomed anew:*
> *Yon looking-glass gleamed at the wave of her feather.*

They have arrived rather late for dinner, on a summer's eve:

> *But 'tis twilight, you see – with such suites to explore,*
> *Such closets to search, such alcoves to importune.*

Browning with his peculiar aromatic stuffiness – his poems seem to me to smell of the inside of cedarwood cigar-boxes – serves as a useful introduction to ex-colonial Shanghai, scene of concessions to the British, French and Americans in the mid-nineteenth century, who imposed on it great monuments of colonial architecture and a gigantic harbour with its installations.

I cross the corridor to visit David and Gregory in their suite, which is even larger than mine, and with a colossal view many storeys down to the street fronting the River Huang-pu, on which there are many ships, and a road bridge, with iron-girdered rusted sides, crossing a tributary. Beyond the bridge there is a park and beyond that high tenement buildings. From their room the view is like a map of the river and harbour, from mine there is the interior of the town, a sea of roofs of a city with a population larger than that of London.

In the morning we are taken to the Temple of the Jade Buddha. We are back in the sequestered world of Tourists and the Shrines They Visit: homing back to the sub-party atmosphere of our international groups – Americans, Japanese, Germans, Overseas Chinese – trailing up stairs to see a seated figure of Buddha – a bit like Prince Albert under the canopy of the Albert Memorial – cut out of a single piece of jade. His date, alas, is 1881; or at any rate in that year he was brought here from Burma by a Chinese monk, and the temple itself was built (originally on another site) in 1882. Maybe he was an antique, but I doubt it, for he looks contemporary with most of the colonial architecture of Shanghai and with the Prince Consort. There is also another, smaller, Buddha, in an unusual reclining posture. Of the things we saw in the Jade Temple, the one I liked most was the beautiful eighteenth-century screen of the Tale of the Sacred Monkey.

We went shopping and to look for presents at the main emporium in Shanghai, a five- or six-storeyed building with many departments, mostly for clothes. It was crowded with people dressed in the dignified dingy clothes of the People's Republic – dusky blue for citizens, dark green for soldiers, with the red star on their caps and red tabs on their uniforms. There were some sailors who struck a lighter note in their white and blue uniforms. David and Gregory bought slippers. I bought a white straw hat. (Later, Gregory told me that I bought a hat every day – and lost it the same day – while we were in China.)

We were taken to a building – once the property of an English family, the Huttons – now the Exhibition Centre for Handicrafts. It has vast galleries with products ranging from screens printed with photogravures of Gainsborough's *Blue Boy* and the Houses of Parliament, to ceramics, lacquer, jade and, finally, straw baskets. It was these last, far the cheapest, products of village industries, which we liked most. Unlike the beautifully made but wholly conventional lacquer and jade artefacts, these are inventive, spontaneous, amusing, suggestive of plea-

sure taken in their making by people who have feelings about animals, plants, vegetables, the things in nature they mimic in straw. Rabbits, hens, pumpkins, pandas, grasshoppers, and a dozen other such, seemed to us the most inventive things here. I bought a basket with a grass-green cicada sitting on the lid. David and Gregory bought many animals.

In the afternoon we went on a tour of the port and the mouth of the Yangtze river. On board the boat there was a party of English ladies who had been attending a congress on flower arrangement in Tokyo. They are to return to London via Canton and Hong Kong. One of them recognized David, and we got into conversation with her. Another said: 'Oh, it all makes me so nostalgic. Last time I was here in 1930, would you believe it, I had several portmanteaux and they were carried into the hotel by five coolies.' I secretly wanted to kiss another lady for referring to the 'good old days before Shanghai was ruined'. Surely, we have been waiting for someone to say this ever since we got here. But these ladies were, I should emphasize, delighted with all they had seen of China.

The Chinese guide of an American group fell over at the foot of a gangway owing, it seemed, to the carelessness of a young American lady who had accidentally pushed him. In an ecstasy of self-reproach she threw herself on him, helped him to his feet, and started rubbing his back remorsefully and unremittingly. She was trying to undo, I felt, all the wrongs done to China in the past by the West.

The river widens and widens, the shores recede, the ships going to sea or coming into harbour space themselves out, ever further apart. Then comes the meeting of the Huang-pu and the Yangtze and the dissolving of everything into sinister yellow spaces, with the silhouettes of ships moving across the just visible line of the horizon.

5 June

We walked into the streets from our hotel this morning and saw dozens of people looking eagerly at a display of ballpoint pens in a shop window. Nearby, there was a shop selling watches. Two of its windows were juxtaposed: in one of them were Chinese watches, in the other Swiss watches. No one looked at the window with the Chinese watches, but there was a crowd around that with the Swiss watches. In a narrow side-street we saw a goose cooped up on the pavement by a wall.

Shop-window displays

After luncheon we were taken to a communal farm outside Shanghai. Going there, we drove through lush, fertile, flat countryside, rice fields, corn, fields of cabbages, all tended with the meticulous care of the Chinese, as though each root, stick, leaf and grain were separately taken care of, tended by hand.

The village was as picturesque as a village in Surrey or Sussex; with a stream running through and a pretty street with old houses, each one different. We stopped at a courtyard with a gate which was the entrance to the headquarters of the commune. A short, energetic, middle-aged man with furrowed cheeks and bright eyes was standing smiling in front of the gate to welcome us. Entering the courtyard we saw a red billboard – with an inscription on it which Mr Lin translated for us: 'Welcome to our English Visitors.'

Our host was deputy director of the commune. He took us up some stone steps to a large room with chairs either side of a table with cups of tea on it, and we sat down. After the usual gracious welcome, he told us this was Lau Tau People's Commune, in which there were 7,417 families. The total population was 25,000. The inhabitants cultivated 2,224 hectares of land (about 5,500 acres).

It operated on three levels: the communal brigades; production brigades; teams. It has 16 production brigades and 146 teams. The chief crops are grain and cotton. Other crops are garlic and rape seed. Cotton, grain and garlic are sold to the state.

There are also animals: pigs. He added that there were white and black mushrooms and white fungus (we had eaten some at luncheon in Shanghai).

The commune also breed fish and cultivate pearls. There are twelve factories which manufacture oxygen, chemicals and parts of electrical apparatus. There is also a lock and key factory and a garage for repairing agricultural machinery. He mentioned copper products and garments, made for export.

The commune has one senior middle school, two junior middle schools and sixteen primary schools.

It has – as we were soon to see – a hospital of its own with a medical staff of 29 and more than 70 beds. The hospital is equipped with an X-ray machine, and electro-cardiograph machinery. The farmers in the commune have their own medical insurance scheme for which they pay 2 yuan a year. All the medical bills of those insured are paid by the commune.

Each production brigade has a clinic with 3 or 4 medical personnel. The average income (arrived at by dividing the whole income of all members of the commune, including babies) is 304 yuan per year. The average annual income of each individual worker is 480 yuan.

The individual member of the commune does not have to pay rent or taxes. But the commune as a whole pays taxes to the state, at the rate of 144 yuan per year per hectare. The tax amounts to 5% of the total income of the whole commune.

After this introduction, which I copied down to the best of my ability (and always with the likelihood that I make mistakes because I seem temperamentally incapable of understanding terms such as 'brigade', cadre' etc.) we were taken to visit the farm. We saw fields of grain, some of which were being harvested, and private allotments – small holdings which belong to the peasants as part of the policy of increasing individual enterprise. Today, we were told, 7% of the whole area of agricultural land consists of these allotments (since writing this, I have read in *The Times* that it has been increased to 15%).

Each family has 60 square metres (72 square yds) of private land which they can cultivate in their spare time and the products of which can be sold in the open market. We were shown pig sties where there were pigs so clean that they looked as if they were scrubbed with soap and water every morning and evening. There were black pigs with black piglets, white pigs with white piglets and – through cross-breeding – black pigs with white and black piglets, white pigs with black and white piglets, demonstrating Mendelian laws.

We were taken next to the hospital and shown the department for Western medicine and that for Chinese medicine. One old woman was there with her grand-daughter who was getting some treatment: but we saw no one who was hospitalized.

Next we were shown a typical ideal home with an ideal family, consisting of ideal husband, ideal wife, ideal mother-in-law and one ideal child inhabiting an ideal living-room-cum-kitchen with an old-fashioned but still ideal stove which burns straw as fuel. There was a bedroom with two large beds. The stove and the saucepans and pots and pans on it were all very clean. This was an old house. Next we

*The deputy director
at the commune:*

were shown a modern house, also ideal. Near these houses there was a bamboo copse, very neat, which went with one or both of them. We were told of the multiple uses to which the householder could put the bamboo.

The owner of the new house explained how he had built it himself. Doing so had cost him altogether 2,000 yuan, 800 of which had gone in various expenses. He still had 1,500 yuan saved which he could bank.

David asked whether children worked in the fields with their parents. Ordinarily, they were not allowed to do so, he was told. 'Are they not allowed to *play* at work then?' David asked disconcertingly. The deputy director conceded that they helped with household chores at home, and they sometimes worked with their parents in the allotments. Also, he went on, the school organized them to help a bit in the fields when the harvest was being gathered.

We went back to the Centre with the deputy director and had luncheon. Every dish was the product of the farm where we had just been. We asked questions about the industrialization of agriculture in China. Under the Four Modernizations emphasis is now being put on tractors, electrification and irrigation. I asked whether it was not possible that if they industrialized agriculture extensively they might create unemployment? The deputy director replied that workers did not necessarily have to work on the land. They could do handicrafts. (We had seen examples

Russian limousine in Shanghai

of such work in showcases as we entered the farm.) He became agitated when David enquired as to how they had reacted on this communal farm when intellectuals were sent away from the towns into the country to do agricultural work. 'Wasn't it a bit of an insult,' David asked, 'to send townspeople who represented 20% of the population to work among the 80% who lived in the country as a form of punishment to the 20%?' The assistant director said it was an insult and the country people resented having these professors sent to work among them.

On our way back to Shanghai we asked Mr Lin whether this commune which seemed so ideal was typical. 'Oh no, by no means,' he answered. 'I only wish it were. It is not typical at all. But it is what we would like communes to be.'

On the boulevard opposite the hotel in Shanghai, young people lingered, attracted there by the activity in the hotel lobby, and anxious to talk to tourists who came out of the hotel. Some spoke English, and David and Gregory started talking with them soon after we arrived in Shanghai. Gregory had made an appointment to go to a café with one of them on this, our last evening in the city, after we had returned from the visit to the commune. While David and I talked in the bar of the hotel, he went off and kept this appointment.

Joining us in the bar later, he said that he had been taken to a café which was crowded with students. The one who had taken him there told him that in order to go to Peking from Shanghai he and his fellow-students had to have permits. There

146

were in fact only one or two places you could visit without one. He himself could not have one because his parents were not Party members. In order to become a Party member your parents must also be members. He said that his brother, aged 17, had got a permit to visit their aunt and uncle in Hong Kong. He had never come back and was now in the U.S.A.

The students thought that another Cultural Revolution was bound to happen. They quoted a saying, current among them: 'Before the Revolution there were notices in hotels for foreigners stating: "Dogs and Chinese not allowed." Today, it is "No Chinese".' Gregory asked one student what would happen if they visited him in our hotel. 'On our way out *they* would approach us and ask for our names and addresses and take them down. *They* are everywhere. Many, many.' The student said that in the evenings he watched TV programmes and read novels. He liked discos but there was no place to dance. Students received 12 yuan a month for going to school.

Employment in hotels was much sought after. There were many people out of work in Shanghai and there had been riots of the unemployed (we had heard about these in Peking). It was nearly impossible for young people to find a place to live. He said, 'In China, the old do not like the young.'

Shanghai students

SS with Mr Li

6 June Kweilin (Guilin)

We arrived here by air from Shanghai. We were met by our local guide, Mr Li, who looked different from our previous guides, sensitive, pale, a transparent complexion, finely drawn features of the kind which make one think of a bone structure underneath carved out of ivory.

He took us to a hotel built on a different plan from any other we had been to, and much pleasanter. Enclosed in a park, it consisted of several one-storeyed or two-storeyed buildings. We are in No. 8. The beds are large and have mosquito nets, the rooms airy and well furnished and not, as elsewhere, all of a pattern. But Gregory later said the beds were uncomfortable, though not as bad as those in Wusih with their hard sheets. Adjoining our apartments there was a dining room with four tables only. The waitresses were exceptionally pretty, and smiling. We were hardly surprised to hear that two or three days previously the king and queen of the Belgians had stayed here.

The meals were served in dishes with food beautifully arranged and harmoniously coloured. David photographed some.

Kweilin: From the moment we stepped out of the aeroplane we could see that it was even more strange and sensational than we had imagined from looking at reproductions of Chinese drawings of craggy landscapes which seem too fantastic to be true.

Scenes in Kweilin

*The plane from
Shanghai to Kweilin*

At the edge of the airfield we already saw a row of palm trees leaning, bent by the wind, and with leaves like scissors, opening and shutting. Beyond them, a sheet of water, beyond that a green plain, and beyond the green plain, rising sheer, hills, each hill separate from the other and each shaped differently. From the moment we first saw them, we fell completely under their spell. As soon as David got to the hotel he started a drawing of hills with hooped outlines filled in with flat colour.

That afternoon we went to two caves. The first, at the edge of the town – and close to the river – contained inscriptions and bas-reliefs of the Buddha carved into the rock. The second was some miles from the town, and a great touristic attraction, on account of its vastness. It was high up among hills. We waited for half an hour at the entrance among the milling tourists, trying not to listen to the Muzak, before being admitted. Having got inside, we saw groups of tourists scattered under the immense vaulted ceiling of the cave, across whose irregular floor paths had been made. The cave was illuminated by floodlight picking out and dramatizing effects produced by stalagmites and stalactites. With its arches, traceries, weird columns, shapes resembling dragons, vegetables, giants etc., it is one of nature's Arthur Rackham-like cathedrals, a nineteenth-century elf-land – but also a twentieth-century refuge from final war. One can well imagine our civilization ending with great crowds taking refuge in enormous underground

vaults, in caves where petrified nature parodies in millennial stone the cathedrals of *Kweilin scenery*
the destroyed civilization.

The voices of guides conducting groups around the immense grotto turned monstrous shapes into metaphors for things in nature. 'Here are toadstools, here, lizards, here an old lady cloaked in lace, here cabbages, here a pineapple, here a dragon.' The monotonous voices did not silence the steady drip drip of water falling from roof to floor, measuring the stony pulse of the thousands of years taken to accomplish change in these surroundings. Listening to the guides, it occurs to me that the cave is like an enormous pair of crocodile jaws with teeth above and below and that finally these will shut tight and the cave become one solid block of rock, with tourists fossilized between the jaws.

That evening I felt ill, so I stayed at the hotel while David and Gregory went to a concert. They described it to me later. It began and ended with extreme abruptness: 'Suddenly, curtains whisked up. Plonk! Show begins. Curtain drop. Plonk! Intermission. Just an announcement to say so. Bell rings, intermission over immediately. Lights go out. End of concert. Nothing to make you believe concert was over, except an announcement to say so.' 'Anyway, one might have known it would end then, because everyone in China is in bed by 10 o'clock,' said Gregory.

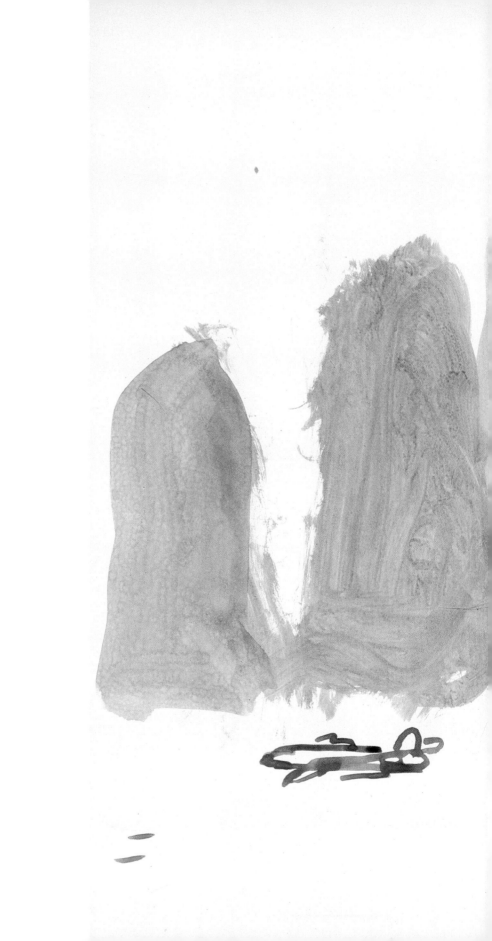

'There was a kind of tenor, a mezzo soprano and a bass. The bass appeared first and sang Mussorgsky's 'Song of a Flea', followed by 'Old Man River' and then a few Yugoslav folk songs. The guide kept on translating them for us. Then the tenor came on, a young man, and he sang to music which was vaguely like Puccini. The guide said it was from films. There was considerable variety. After the tenor, music from the national minorities. After that, *Carmen*, the "March of the Toreadors".' Gregory: 'That was very good.' David: 'It was tremendously fast, but it was interesting to watch.' Gregory: 'What was very popular near the end was a boy and girl who sang songs in which there was a lot of laughter: "Hee Hee Hee Hee Hee . . ." The audience was delighted, the sound was very pleasing and these two got the most applause.'

David said he had the impression that traditional music was mostly from the opera and theatre in China. For some reason, there was, apart from the opera, very little folk music. In fact, Mr Lin had told him there was more folk music among the national minorities.

David and Gregory agreed that the best instrumentalist was a woman drummer who was quite wonderful. But while pounding on the drums, she showed no emotion whatever. David said: 'Normally drummers go berserk. They're giving it a real beat and rhythm. They're the most energetic performers in the orchestra. But she showed absolutely no emotion whatever. Marvellous really. Never seen anything quite like it. She'd do really well in Harlem; it would be something entirely new.'

They told me that during the interval, the young guide from Kweilin, Mr Li, had asked them what they thought about the Beatles, explaining that in China that kind of music is discouraged. The Chinese, he said, considered it immoral. David liked Mr Li, whom he thought the most intelligent and interesting guide we had had, a real person who wanted to enter into a real conversation with him. Mr Li asked: 'How can you like that kind of music, when you have Chopin and Beethoven?' David told me: 'I said the point about music is whether it has life. Jazz is full of vitality. If music doesn't have life it's soon forgotten. It's not the particular style that matters, but the degree of vitality. The best of jazz will last because people understand it, feel the force . . .'

Mr Li then said that corrupt Western music was just a passing fashion, and this had reminded David of a *Times* leader which appeared after the death of Elvis Presley: 'It said that Elvis was a bit of a hype, his reputation was a con put on by managers. . . . It's odd that the English should take this view; though in doing so, they're being like the Chinese official Party member who takes really the same view – essentially an unbelievably false view of culture, I think. That deep contempt for people – that most people are cheap, nothing, that's the view. I do not hold that view myself.'

David said that he began to see points about the Cultural Revolution we had not been told about: that it was in part the rebellion of the young who had ideas of their own and who did not have the great adventure of the Long March behind them, as against the older generation of bureaucrats. He thought that what had gone wrong with the Cultural Revolution was the chauvinism, its being directed – largely through the influence of the Gang of Four and in accordance with traditional Chinese xenophobia – against the outside world, which it ought to have reached out to, and let in. I said that the students in Paris had, indeed, thought of the Chinese Red Guards as part of their international movement. How wrong they had been! David said: 'What Mao should have done – this is right, I am sure – is open up things in China to the world. That he didn't do so was a mistake and it soon resulted in new chauvinism – the Gang of Four – fighting with old chauvinism.'

We told Mr Lin about the conversation which David and Gregory had with Mr Li about music. Mr Lin, however, was insistent that there was no official government policy regarding taste in music and the arts. He said: 'What you heard was the opinion of one person, which I also overheard a bit of. These are only his opinions absolutely. I am more official than he is. I am a government official. I do not fully agree with him; we have different opinions. So in this sense we are still in the process of debate. I don't think the authorities are trying to decide about popular music, they can't – they know they can't decide that. You may notice that people go in the public park with tape recorders, playing this popular music in the parks. I myself don't like it, but we don't prohibit it. This disco music, where does it come from? From Hong Kong. People bring it into China and distribute it to those who can afford to buy it. If it's good, then I think that after twenty years, thirty years, it will be remaining with the people. So don't have the impression that the authorities are trying to prohibit it.' He was extremely emphatic.

7 June

Today we went on the famous trip down the Li River, for six hours, to Yang Shuo.
We were on a pretty boat with a large cabin and a deck shaded by a red and yellow
awning. The other tourists were Overseas Chinese, Americans, Brazilians. As soon
as we left Kweilin a lady guide started bawling at us through a loudspeaker to look
at the rock across the river on our right – could we see an elephant's foot? (or ear?
or trunk? – I forget what). After a few moment's silence in which we presumably
took banal poetry of nature in, she went on to inform us that the first third of the
journey was not interesting. David muttered that, as far as he was concerned, he
was sure it would be the most interesting part. In a sense she was right. It wasn't.
For the first part of the journey those strange hills were a mile or so distant from us
on each side of the populous plain through which the river runs. But as we went
further downstream the landscape became less inhabited, with feathery clumps of
bamboo skirting its banks. There were occasional villages with fishing boats on the
water or drawn up on the shore. We saw a road along one side of the river. Soon it
could be seen no more. The river narrowed. The plain on each side of the river
stopped, the hills drew nearer, and the river was flanked by the lower slopes of the
miniature mountains behind them. Soon there was nothing between the river banks

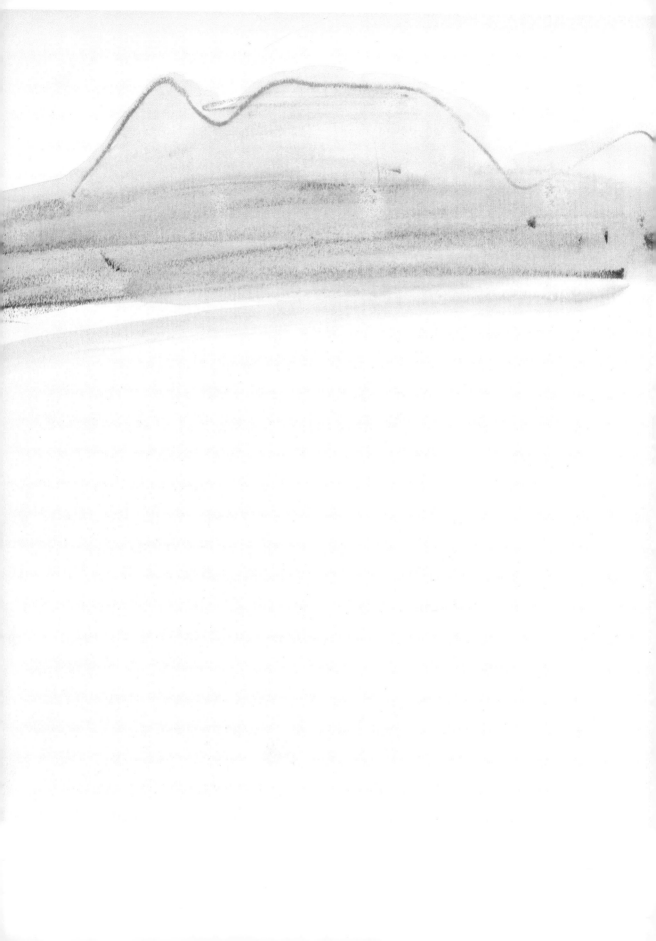

and those hills except, on each side, the narrowest strip of flat green on which, at intervals, solitary farmhouses or the clustered walls and roofs of minute villages were visible.

Suddenly, beyond two points of wooded shore, in front of us, round a bend in the river, those dream-like hills came right down to us on both sides of the water, very close to our launch, as though we could reach out and touch them. Some were enveloped in foliage from top to bottom, hazy, golden, or the bright green, slightly sickly colour of verdigris. Others were gashed, stripped of shrubs and grass right down their sides, where the rock was scarred bare, gleaming, flesh-coloured, streaked from top to bottom with ink-black lines, drawn crossways and downways by the weather which had also stained and blotched them. Looking at a rocky outcrop which pointed like a finger, upwards, with a mould of green foliage where the finger nail should be, and lines running —own it, David said: 'You can see the ink running down the paper.'

I saw gushing through the shrubby lower slopes of the hills, a seven-branched waterfall of separate silver threads, like a candelabra held upside down, and the water spreading in lines on horizontal ledges of the river bank, then spilling over in one solid sheet down into the river.

Standing on the deck of the boat as it followed the bends in the river, we found, when we tried to take photographs, that the scenes framed in our viewfinders twisted and turned round just when we had focused on them, as though the hills were a formation of crystals held in the palm of a revolving hand.

For an hour or so we were steered into a magical world where nature had become visual music. Then the hills receded again. The shore spread out its wide flat green aprons of land on either side between us and them.

During the short voyage among the hills everyone on the launch had become infected with a strange exhilaration. An American geologist, a bearded bespectacled keen young professorial type, with two or three younger people, perhaps his students, delivered a lecture to them, on the formation of these limestone rocks.

Also on the boat were a couple of Chinese (they too must have been Overseas Chinese) dressed in People's Army uniform; or rather the top half of each was in uniform. Both the man and the woman wore the jackets of officers in the People's Army, complete with red tabs, but made of exceptionally elegant material, probably in Hong Kong. She wore a blue silk shirt and carried a smart shoulder bag which she waved about a lot from side to side. These two never stopped photographing one another, jumping about on deck to find suitable backgrounds, parodying us more serious photographers. I wondered what right they had to be dressed in this way and wanted very much to ask Mr Lin, but refrained from doing so partly from fear of arousing some disciplinary conscience in him which would make him command them to go below deck and change their clothes – or to have them put in irons perhaps – partly because he might in any case become greatly upset. Mr Lin

The professor on the boat

had, I thought, when they walked his way, an expression on his face as though he was deliberately ignoring some grave affront to the order of things in China.

On the trip with us there was also a Chinese professor, brought along by Mr Lin, and, I think, formerly a teacher of our young Kweilin guide. He was a distinguished looking man, with greying hair, very pale complexion, dark hollow eye-sockets in which the eyes were an almost cornflower blue, and had a worn air of sadness about him. He wore a pale-blue suit and looked like a Picasso Blue Period boy grown old.

I asked him about his work at the university, and he told me that, during the Cultural Revolution, he had had to sweep the floors, after having made a confession of political guilt. I asked him whether he found it repugnant to confess. He replied, with a wan smile, 'Oh no, there is always a lot to confess.' He said that when he was not cleaning the building he was being given lessons in Maoism by the students He did not seem to resent all this, but found it, in the Chinese way, in retrospect something faintly giggly, or at any rate to be related with a smile. He also attended the concert when David and our guide discussed Western popular music, which he seemed to find immoral also. In fact all his views seemed orthodox.

On reaching Yang Shuo, we disembarked on the river bank; it was a touristy resort, quite ostentatiously picturesque. Shops and stalls here, open onto the street, gushed with the kumquats, pommelos, persimmons, chestnuts, mangosteen and other products for which the town is famous. The free market seemed to contain nothing but vegetables, fruit, Chinese medicines and souvenirs. There was little traffic except for arriving and departing charabancs, and the whole town was a promenade for tourists.

We walked around a bit and then got into the minibus which had been sent by the hotel to meet us. To go back to Kweilin on the river and against the stream would have taken seven hours. The road on which we drove went through lush green wet fields, flat emerald mirrors traversed by ditches for irrigation, above which at various distances we saw the hills shaped like chimneys, triangular sails, fins of sharks, sugar loaves, kilns, singly or in clusters, thrusting up from the perfectly smooth plain.

Cypresses, Chinese poplars and other trees, each of them separate and looking like detailed drawings or engravings of themselves, also stood out above the fields, strange and distinct. David asked the driver to stop the minibus. In fields, he photographed trees. While he was doing so, a peasant who was by the roadside came up and stood stock still looking at me and the guides. He fingered the blade of a pruning knife which he held in his hands. Neither of our guides seemed aware of his presence, or looked at, or smiled at him. I kept turning to see whether he was still there and not as invisible as their obliviousness to him seemed to imply.

I was feverish throughout the night and had what I can only describe as a political nightmare, of a kind I had already experienced once in Peking. I dreamed that I had to write a poem in traditional form about a classical subject, Anchises. At first I felt extremely excited about this. I thought I would write about some subject very immediate to me and yet sublimate it within the traditional classical subject and in some metre which I had never attempted. It seemed to me a matter of life or death whether I would succeed in doing this. After a time, a gap seemed to widen between idea and form, like a space that I could not fill. Besides, I had forgotten who Anchises was. I could not breathe, I felt that I was going to die. Even when I woke I had the sense of something deeply, even terribly, unsatisfactory, this failure on my part to perform a task, and the inability to fill a space between the wish to do something and the conditions under which it could be done.

*Scenes on the road between
Yang Shuo and Kweilin*

8 June

In the morning Mr Lin came to my room and said he was very concerned about me. As on several occasions before, I was made aware of his great natural kindness (David and Gregory were also made aware of it at other times). I had really felt ill during the night, but to my surprise I could tell him that I was quite recovered.

We were taken to see Tang A-hsi, an artist aged $8\frac{1}{2}$, Tang A-chin, his sister, aged 7, and their parents. They lived in a small house on the edge of a little lake just outside Kweilin. Quite apart from the interest of the child prodigy, this was an occasion for us, our first visit to a Chinese home. For I do not count the show piece of the Communal Farm.

The area where the Tang family lived was a settlement of small houses with gardens and front and back yards. It was neighbourly. Footpaths between houses were scrawled with graffiti by the children. These were mostly of aeroplanes, ships and guns, but I noticed that one was of Buddha.

The Tang family home consisted of a tiny front room, a living room and two bedrooms. All these were small. There was also a tiny kitchen. The floors were concrete, uncarpeted, the furniture sparse. In the living room there were three children's miniature chairs and three large ones for adults. There was a small round table and a tiny square one. In the parents' bedroom, onto which the living room opened, there was a bed and a large clothes cupboard, on top of which was a suitcase. Also, on a table a TV set and a small radio.

In the front room the 8-year-old artist worked at a table consisting of a board supported by two packing cases. Lighting was supplied by two naked bulbs hanging by wires from the ceiling.

(It is, I know, impertinent to go into people's houses and describe them in this way, which may well seem patronizing, but the Western reader has no basis of comparing standards of living without such seizing on of opportunities to observe things. I apologize to the little boy and his family if ever they should read this.)

The living room was brightened by specimens of the boy's watercolours, his sister's calligraphy and one or two pictures by his father hung on the wall. Some of the young prodigy's paintings were of the famous limestone hills rising from the water, which we have seen the day before. In the pictures there were many boats on the river. Other pictures were of cats, or kittens. These seemed to be jumping out of the paper to play around the room with the artist and his sister. There were also, I remember, two or three framed drawings by their father and a framed certificate (the boy had won a prize in a competition for young artists). We were shown a reproduction of his prize-winning picture in the exhibition catalogue.

At first the child prodigy sat without any expression on his face – or perhaps a rather glum one – as though he were unaware of our presence. His sister sat beside him in her little chair, equally unforthcoming. We felt embarrassed on their behalf. Why should they be made a show of?

Their father, rather apologetic, explained that the children were not yet properly awake. Then the children were given cups of some beverage which they held in their hands and occasionally sipped. Meanwhile their father supplied us with statistics. His son had begun painting when he was six. His average rate of production was two paintings per day. He had (then) a total oeuvre of 9,000 pictures. We were handed examples of his work, very small pictures, about 3″ by 2″, pasted onto sheets of paper.

These miniatures showed a child's imagination, as well as being the work of quite an accomplished painter, done with assurance. David at once saw the point of the pictures, not so much the landscapes as of the cats. 'He's the most interesting painter we've seen yet in China. He knows exactly what he's doing. Naturally he doesn't want to bother with us.'

His father now coaxed the boy to the table, set a rather rumpled sheet of paper down on it, and encouraged him to start painting. His mother, who had frizzy hair and a shy smile, stood near him, murmuring encouragement. The little girl sat herself down at her small table and started doing calligraphy.

At first the boy gave the paper a disgusted look, then he picked up a brush, dipped it in water and paint and drew a form resembling the hull of a submarine. Then, working outwards from this as centre, he sketched in rocks and boats. He stood

up while he brushed in their forms in broad strokes. Then he signed to his father to *Domestic exterior*
bring him a chair, and took up a fine brush drew in details of the boats.

David produced from Gregory's canvas bag a box of crayons and presented them to A-hsi. Laying his hand flat on the crayons in their box with the lid open, the boy counted them, one by one. There were thirty. He smiled blissfully at David. From that moment, it was as though the two of them were at one, children or artists, or both. David now produced from the same magical canvas bag two drawing books, one a solid block of sheets gummed together at one end, from which you tear off the top sheet when you have finishing using it, the other an ordinary book. Childish, the boy was just as fascinated by the novelty of tearing off the sheets from the block as later he was by a metal holder David gave him for clasping chalks; and, still later, by spray fixative.

Each time David gave him a piece of apparatus he would gaze at it with bright eyes from his brown and elfin face under the black matted hair, as though he wanted to play with holder or spray, just for its own sake. But then when David showed him how to use it as part of the process of drawing, his expression would change and he'd start working with it quite professionally.

David drew a rocky Kweilin hill in the sketchbook, which was better than the block for working in crayon. He showed him how with these crayons you can first

draw pencilled lines, like shading, then with a water-loaded brush make them into a wash. He also showed how you can superimpose washes of colour on one another; and how with a penknife you can scratch lines into the layers of paint once they are dry and hard. While painting, David explained in English what he was doing. Although the child did not understand a word of English, he grasped at once the sense of what was being said, by David's demonstration. The boy watched David doing all this intently and could scarcely wait to seize the crayons and try himself. Really, he grasped the technique immediately.

David said afterwards: 'He is absolutely an artist. He was excited by having the new materials and immediately got the hang of how to use them.'

With the crayons the boy drew the outline of a hill, filled it in with lines drawn diagonally, and then brushed water into the lines, turning the colour into a wash. David then drew a bicycle which was leaning on a fence opposite the window, and gave it to the boy, who clasped David's hand. They were two artists together.

Meanwhile in the living room the little girl (whom David had also presented with crayons and drawing books) was happily at work with her calligraphy. As happens in China, people began appearing from everywhere – an elderly woman who was perhaps the children's grandmother, a tall lank man who looked like a schoolteacher and two or three other children.

The boy then drew pictures of kittens for each of us – two for David, a solitary one for me – and his sister did a large pink watery calligrammatic squiggle for David.

The cats were laid across the backs of chairs to dry. The boy went outside into the yard, taking with him his crayon drawing of the rocks and joyfully sprayed it with fixative. With one thumb he rubbed a patch of colour to check that it was fixing properly, and David had to explain that he must wait till it was completely dry, or it would smudge. David took Polaroid photographs outside in the yard, and distributed them as largesse. As we left he and his fellow-artist walked, hand in hand, as far as our cars.

At lunch I remarked: 'He completely changed, didn't he, when he realized that you were also a painter?' David said: 'Yes, it was extraordinary, the change that came over him.' Then he added: 'Both of them, they completely lit up, didn't they? I can remember, you know, proud parents who watch their child and then say: "Do a drawing for Uncle Willy", but the child doesn't really want to do any such thing. But the moment he began drawing he didn't mind, did he? Just goes into it, doesn't matter whether we're there or not. The cats have the most feeling of life in them, don't they?' he said, speaking about the drawings.

He felt confident that the boy would become a really good artist. I said that if he did just cats his observation of the real cats in the house might become exhausted and the drawing become mechanical, like so much modern Chinese art we had seen.

Restaurant

David said: 'All children draw by looking first and then making the drawing. The subject doesn't have to be in front of him for a child to draw. Whatever cats he draws, they are the cats in the house that he sees playing, which he looks at with joy. His work is obviously based on his feeling for them. He loves them.'

Mr Lin told us that a TV programme had been made of the little boy at work. I said: 'The danger is they will make him a tourist attraction.' David said, 'I don't think they will, because he'll resist it. That's why he sulked when we first arrived. He is like that. He's saying: "Leave me alone." But in the Chinese way you do what your parents tell you to in the end. The little girl didn't want to do anything. I watched her in her corner. The moment the boy realized we had something to give him to do with his work, there was a complete change.'

I said it was extraordinary how completely happy he became. And David added, 'and he grabbed my hand and sat down and enjoyed drawing. He understood, he watched everything, he learned immediately. The girl, she was as fast in observing. All artists learn from watching someone work. When I was a student in art school, we learned most from watching other students. You're in the same room, and they're painting away, and you see a lot of things.'

In the evening we were taken to a poetry recital given in our honour at the Teachers' Training Centre. This was a large concrete building, unattractive

The Teachers' Training College

inside. We could not judge the outside as it was dark when we arrived, rather late. We were rushed through the preliminary reception ceremonies, and had scarcely time for a sip of the tea provided, before being guided to our allotted places in the front row of a lecture theatre with tiered seats. Written in chalk on the blackboard, in copperplate roman lettering, was the legend 'Poetry Recital'. On either side of this was a drawing in purple chalk of a floating sylph, a pre-Raphaelite figure like book illustrations by Walter Crane. We were welcomed in a short speech by Dr Ho. Then someone gave me a bunch of gardenias, which I held in front of me, sniffing at them occasionally, for the rest of the evening.

After the welcoming speech, a member of the faculty who looked like a young snub-nosed bronze-cheeked subaltern read a long poem in English welcoming this poet and this painter coming from the land of Shakespeare, Spenser, Milton, Keats, etc. I tried to memorize his opening lines. They ran something like this:

> *Welcome to you, friends from England,*
> *Flowers beautiful in hand,*
> *Welcome, from remote Northern origin,*
> *And West Europe, . . .*

Their manner of reading aloud seemed based on Chinese opera, acted out recitative perhaps, with gestures, pauses, inviting smiles, voice suddenly raised and then suddenly dropped. The flower-like girls can only be described as pirouetting, with inviting smiles, through their lines. Any opportunity to imitate a call or sound from nature was exploited to the utmost: 'cuckoo, cuckoo, cuckoo,' trilled a girl, hand to ear and eyes looking sidelong, as she evoked Wordsworth's cuckoo.

The young man who read Shelley's 'Ode to the West Wind' (banned during the Cultural Revolution for not being the East Wind – in fact suspected of being the Ode to the CIA Wind) was of rather ferocious aspect, a bit like one of those colourful generals who are guardians of the outer shrines of Buddhist temples – at once fierce and benign. He seemed quite aware of the humour of his performance and occasionally broke into an involuntary charming smile, diminishing his ferocity considerably when he did this. The audience responded with a titter. The West Wind, though officially rehabilitated, disintegrated rather under his treatment.

From where I sat I could see, through the window at my side, figures of young men standing and looking in from the shrubbery and being much persecuted by mosquitoes, which they dealt with unhesitatingly. They gaped with unconcealed delight and with nudgings and whisperings at the poetic gesturings of the prettier among the nervous girls within. Gazing out of shrubby darkness at girls reciting foreign poetry seemed a pleasure rare enough in China. It demolished frontiers.

Chinese poems were translated into English and, apart from the last one which, though written in the year 1001, might have been written in the present century by Yeats, seemed as Romantic as the poems written by the English. It is extraordinary, I reflected, the conquest of Asia – India most of all – by the English Romantic poets. Perhaps there is something oriental about the Romantic imagination – the beginning of what in the early nineteenth century Goethe called World Literature. But influences are reciprocal: Asia finds its way into Romantic poetry in Shelley's *Prometheus Unbound* and in Coleridge's 'Kubla Khan', which is about Kweilin, is it not?

> *Where Alph, the sacred river ran*
> *Through caverns measureless to man*
> *Down to a sunless sea.*

A poem about following the path laid down by Chairman Mao and with the raised banners of the Four Modernizations triumphantly entering the twenty-first century was read next but, I noted, was applauded only in perfunctory fashion. One had the feeling: 'It's already too late for this kind of thing.'

I was asked to 'recite and lecture', so I read a poem of six lines called 'Word':

WORD

The word bites like a fish.
Shall I throw it back free
Arrowing to that sea
Where thoughts lash tail and fin?
Or shall I pull it in
To rhyme upon a dish?

I also repeated some of the thoughts I have expressed here about Asia and English Romanticism. I said: 'I hope that, together with the Four Modernizations, China will become open to the movement in modern poetry in the English language in this century which began with W. B. Yeats: and that I thought the best message I could give them was simply to write on the blackboard, three names: W. B. Yeats, T. S. Eliot, W. H. Auden.

The evening ended with thanks and the collective singing of Auld Lang Syne.

9–11 June   Canton (Guangzhou)

From Kweilin we took a morning flight to Canton. We regarded Canton, where we were to spend two days only, as a stop intermediary to our returning to the Peninsula Hotel in Hong Kong, before we separated – David and Gregory to Los Angeles, I to Athens. A bit ashamed, we admitted to each other that we were looking forward to the fleshpots of Hong Kong. To analyze why we felt this would throw light on our feelings about China and certainly on the feelings of a great many Cantonese about Hong Kong: for 80% of the population of Canton have relations in Hong Kong, Mr Lin told us, and receive gifts from them. Mr Lin warned us that Canton was dangerous. We might, at the very least, have our pockets picked. There is certainly a feeling about Canton as though the fuel of Marxist-Leninist-Maoist thought burns low here. To us, it seemed far more like the West than anywhere else we had been in China.

Canton seemed less a world city, less affected by a kind of international gigantism, than Shanghai; it is more European, with its boulevards, public gardens, streets with arcades. Much of it was built during the 1920s as part of a great scheme of slum clearance. Under the arcades, there are shops full of goods and bustling with activity, reminding one perhaps not so much of Paris or London as of those cities

The word BITES like
A FISH

Shall I throw it back, FREE
Arrowing to that sea

Where thoughts lash tail and FIN
Or shall I pull it in

To rhyme upon a dish

when they are translated into their Middle Eastern or North African version: Cairo or Beirut or Casablanca. Canton is in the forefront of the Chinese government's experiments in free enterprise.

We stayed in a hotel which was next to one of the large Friendship Stores reserved for foreigners or privileged Chinese in possession of 'funny money', and to which we were regularly taken in towns in China. After putting our things down in our hotel rooms, we went to explore it. We noticed that two men, standing rather unobtrusively at the entrance, scrutinized everyone who entered the store. They stopped one young man and would not let him in: evidently a Chinese who had no right to enter, with or without 'funny money', like the young man in Sian who had asked us to buy cigarettes for him.

I left David and Gregory, who had decided to buy some rhinoceros- and antelope-horn pills, and walked back alone the few yards to the hotel. On my way, a woman standing on the pavement with an emaciated child in her arms offered to sell me lychees. I bought a bunch. The moment I took out my wallet to pay the price she had asked, she asked twice as much. I quickly paid her, took the lychees and hurried off. For some reason I was scared of the beggar in a country where, officially at least, there are supposed to be none.

We told Mr Lin that we insisted on walking about the town rather than go sightseeing. We went only to the five-storeyed museum called the Pavilion, a fourteenth-century building overlooking the sea (in fact, today it overlooks a stadium with multiple lights on top of poles). It is a dark-brown building sandwiched between jutting eaves separating each storey so that it looks like cards stacked on top of one another to make a house of cards. This is a historic museum beginning on the ground floor with finds from archaeological digs in the neighbourhood, then ascending to China's earliest contacts with European merchants on the next floor, continuing upwards to anti-European movements in China, and thence to the Communist revolution. I found myself fascinated by the photographs of the events of 1911 – Sun Yat-sen and Yuan Shi-kai. The examples and documentation in the museum were very well displayed – though, of course, always in a partisan way so that all past events are seen as pointing towards the glorious triumph of communism. Since the appeal of this propaganda is at least partly directed towards the foreign visitor, it seems a pity that all the captions are given only in Chinese.

I wrote in my room in the hotel that first evening. David and Gregory wanted to explore the town. Mr Lin, unwilling to let them face the dangers of Canton alone, took them to the Park of Culture and Rest. This sounded improving and educative, so that I did not altogether envy them the experience, but they came back tremendously excited. The next evening, I went there with them in order to see for myself.

It was dark when we got to the park, since David had insisted on giving our guides dinner at what was supposedly the best restaurant in Canton. This was a building of several storeys, and we dined with our Chinese guests in a banqueting room by ourselves. Two storeys below, there was a Chinese wedding, and at the

height of the festivities we could hardly hear ourselves speak for the noise of fireworks.

Mr Lin on a Shanghai bus

The park contained a multiplicity of shows – immensely varied – theatre, opera, cinema, basketball and other activities all going on separately, side by side, simultaneously. In addition to these, there were the ferris wheel and other features of an amusement park. The first show we saw was of scenes from Chinese opera. When we arrived, a duet was going on between a man and a woman, both of them dressed in everyday clothes, on a stage on which was seated a small orchestra. There was no scenery. Of course, I could not understand what they were saying, but the Chinese near-recitative (not quite recitative because there was a long drawn out, spacious, rather monotonous melody, a rhythm like the swaying of a very slow pendulum) suggested to me some leisured pastoral scene, the rather coy conversation of a shepherd and shepherdess. In the manner of pastoral modes, there was something calm and clear about it which made me feel I could go on listening for ever. Even though I had not the slightest idea what the words meant, a rhythm corresponding to words, somewhat like the following, went through my mind:

HE

I met you here upon a summer morning
You plucked a blossom from a bough and threw it at me

Mr Lin with
giant masks

SHE
The petals broke their snowflakes on your face

HE
I did not know whether to smile or weep

At this point, I thought, humming the tune to myself and improvising the speeches, there would be, in Western opera, mounting excitement, some kind of climax would be attained. They would have made declarations of love or parted in tears. But the Chinese singers continued with their conversation in this eternal way as though their eyes, averted from one another, were looking at some third object, say an apple, while they went on singing.

We walked on a few yards and then came to a roller-skating rink where there were many young people. Next we came to a basketball game. Mr Lin pushed us forward and found ringside seats for us where we sat at the edge of the brightly lit oblong space on which the athletes of two teams, pinks and blues, were playing. They were light-footed prancing giants moving from end to end of the field scoring or failing to score goals. From where I sat watching them in the dark, the players seemed like giant moths with wings that were limbs rushing frantically between dizzying opposite goals which beckoned them like candle flames.

A very curious thing happened on our first evening in Canton – of no significance, I am sure, except for the lingering sense it left of strangeness. When David and Gregory got back from walking in the streets of Canton, a near-disaster had happened. Their bathroom floor had been flooded due to a tap being left on, wetting a suitcase in which there was photographic material. Later we discovered that the room of a guest on the floor below had also been flooded. The water supply in the hotel was turned off every day between 4 p.m. and 7 p.m. No one in the hotel had told guests that this was going to happen although there was a service desk with attendants on each floor of the hotel. On the following evening, I noticed that two other bathrooms on our floor were similarly overflowing. People had turned on the taps and, no water coming out, had forgotten to turn them off. Rather to David's amusement, I said to Mr Lin: 'I can't imagine any hotel any-where else where someone on the staff would not have warned the guests that the water was turned off between four and seven; or failing to do that, would not have sent an employee along to see whether any taps had been left running.' It was the only occasion, on our journey, David said, when Mr Lin looked baffled and could not think of anything to say.

On our last morning in China, Mr Lin took us to the Canton railway station to catch the through train to Hong Kong. When we got to the customs barrier, he said, rather solemnly, I thought, 'Here my powers end. From beyond that barrier you are on your own.' This reminded me of some guardian spirit in a masque who accompanies and protects the hero through the forest and then has to leave him.

Private enterprise in Canton

Before this, he had stated, with feeling, that he had really enjoyed being with us and we could certainly say that we too had enjoyed his company. He also told us that the Travel Bureau had considered our trip to China very carefully and had decided that we would not wish to meet anyone official. David said, 'They were quite right.' I agreed, but was left wondering who really were the artists and poets we had met, and who really are the poets and artists we did not meet, if there are any left.

Our last glimpse of the People's Republic of China, at the border with Hong Kong, was of two very young customs officers seated on one chair with their arms around each other. It suddenly struck the note of innocence that we found, for example, in the guide at Kweilin, and the young people walking along the covered corridor of the Summer Palace.

Hong Kong did not prove to be the great release that we had imagined it would be. On the contrary, we felt rather lost there, our minds preoccupied by memories. We went to a drugstore to find medicine for my bronchitis. While we were waiting for it David suddenly exclaimed, 'Well, we've said goodbye to those dear sweet Chinese.' I was left wondering.

Mr Lin

Epilogue

Extracts from a conversation between David Hockney and Stephen Spender, Los Angeles, 9 January 1982.

DH . . . The trip the three of us made was an extremely pleasant and thrilling three weeks, to me, anyway; and it was an experience that you would never forget. Suddenly, this vast country that hardly existed before, except in your imagination, was there. You go there with one idea, to write about it, and I to draw it. I soon realized that it wasn't too easy because of time. We had a very organized day; our only free time was meals, our only time alone was usually dinner. We tended to go to bed early, as everybody did in China, sometimes at 8 p.m. Then we got up at 6 and the day was off again. Soon, I found that I did not quite know how to record in drawings all that was crammed into each day, so I fell back on using the camera. In Peking I was still trying to draw. By the time we got to Nanking I realized I couldn't do it in my way; it wasn't just the organization of the trip, but the lack of time. And I found out too that it wasn't easy to be a journalistic artist.

Often artists choose to go to places because they think it will interest them, or they *know* it will interest them. I first came to L.A. on a hunch that I would find it visually interesting. My hunch was correct. I went to Egypt with a little hunch that it would be interesting, and it was. I visited Nuremberg once, but I never thought it would interest me visually, and it didn't; other things did about it, the area – I'd been visiting Bayreuth. A medieval city is unstimulating to me, whereas to others it might be a great turn-on. It's just what you see in it. I had no notion at all about China. What I have to do now is to sit back and think quietly. Certainly, I was visually most affected by Kweilin, but I think almost any artist would be: very stunning, strange, beautiful landscape. You'd have to have dull eyes not to be fascinated and moved by it. But Peking seemed dull to me. Sian, the city itself, seemed dull, but the hotel building seemed a little more interesting and I actually made a little watercolour of it from memory. The diggings were interesting to us, intellectually and visually. If you are writing about Hangchow, when you discover that what you thought was 200 years old turns out to be 20, that's interesting. And if they did it only a few years ago, why didn't they do it in another way?

SS Well, they seem to have only two ways: the Stalinist way, which was Peking, and the completely traditional way, as in the jade and lacquer factories.

DH What I don't know is how visual a book we should make it. That depends on what I make of the ideas, in the end. It should be like a patchwork diary.

When we arrived in Peking, we sat for dinner on that rather grubby balcony with the British Council Representative. I sat looking at the park, facing outwards, and, to me, it was like the lake in Peel Park, Bradford; nothing very beautiful, compared to, say, a European spa; it seemed dusty and grubby. By the time we had been there three days, you felt a certain deadness; everybody seemed docile. We mentioned this to the British Ambassador, and Mr Hunter sensed that we were a bit disappointed and he said to me, this isn't China; you just wait, it will be a lot more exciting. He was right. Was that experience a real one? Did we miss a great deal in Peking? We never got behind those walls to see the little houses where people lived. If you go to any city in India you see all that and it makes it more interesting. In India you never feel deadness. Isn't that what we have to deal with? We can't pretend that we didn't get it – that feeling of deadness. We don't know what we missed, frankly. Even people who have lived there a long time have never got to know the country better. Many books which come out on China tell you too much: they try to tell you the things they don't really know.

SS What visual ideas do you think you need for the book?

DH I have given up the idea of its being illustrational; I gave that up in China. It has to be put together as one thing, text and images. Reading your diary is like looking at the photographs we took. And the more we think about it, the more we can make something personal out of it, which of course makes it much more interesting to other people. There are so many personal and telling details. In Peking, we travelled about in a little Japanese bus, as in most of the other places, the kind of bus that you would find in London or L.A.; when we got on the train it was like another period altogether, completely different, little lace tablecloths, little pots of flowers; the hotels, the ways they differed. I even remember the sheets in the hotel in Sian, where the beds were very uncomfortable; so they were in Kweilin where there was no mattress. The rooms were dark. The hotel in Sian was semi-Stalinist. When we drove in, I even rather liked the strange little lobby. Then there is the marvellous scene in the hotel in Canton, with the bath tub overflowing. That should be in, because it couldn't happen anywhere else. It only happened because of their strange way of cutting off the water.

SS I have an idea someone did say, don't have a bath between 4 and 7!

DH They cut the water off daily. When Mr Lin came up to me and said, 'You've left the water on,' I thought, oh my God, they're going to think it's terrible, it's probably never happened before in this hotel. But you got upstairs and you realized it's the hundredth time it's happened that week. It's little personal experiences like this that will make it interesting.

SS Yes, you are quite right: this book is about *our* trip and I think I should make it more so by editing and breaking it up. And we have three kinds of illustration arising from the text: literal background photographs, so that you're surrounded by the real photographic reality; illustrations of its being our trip, for instance, pictures that describe what you look like, what I look like, what Gregory looks like, what Mr Lin looks like, what occasional people we met look like. Then, there is a third kind, your own contribution which stands outside, which is really your own vision of China, quite independent of the text.

DH   We went through a giant country that we knew very little about. So we can't make pronouncements on it. . . .

SS   Each of us has a separate personality. I think about China in my own way. I forget about you, and you as David Hockney think about it and illustrate it and have a picture in your mind which is unique to you, your sort of unique vision which is beyond me. Just as you have your unique vision of California which no one else has at all. I think this should be clear at every point in the book.

DH   As I said, it was hard to keep drawing all the time. The difficulty I had, as we rushed round to so many places, so many things, was that I never realized quite the speed with which we would travel. If I had known that, or if we made the journey again, I would have adapted myself to very speedy drawing, which I never got round to because it would have taken another week to re-invent another style of doing it; and for some reason I kept imagining we'd have a half hour or an hour to spend and I'd do this. I imagined it would be like when I went to Egypt; but there I stayed in one particular place, walked around and drew. In China, this was not the case; it was very difficult. So what I will have to do now, by re-living it through the text and the photographs, is to find a new technique of making more drawings.

There are four main characters – you, me, Gregory and Mr Lin. So there should be portraits of us all, as there will be photographs of us all. Some other characters come in vividly, some don't. Take Mr Lin, for instance; he has begun to live again in my mind. . . .

Images begin to come stronger to me: they are not the landscapes, necessarily; they are little details that add up. The difference between the Toyota bus and the still-life on the train has meaning. But there are also neutral areas which don't fit categories. For instance, take architecture: it could be Stalinist, or traditionalist, or neutral, like the diplomats' quarter and the Friendship Stores! . . . There was also a neutral side to Mr Lin, as there was to other things: food; Canton itself – oddly enough, in Chinese terms, a neutral area, a new economic zone. The categories begin to shift.

SS   The neutral way of seeing Mr Lin would be as someone like Leopold Bloom, wandering through China!

DH   It's a very good idea. . . . Everything's a little more complex: the plastic seats versus the lovely silk in the train; the lacquer factory; the little boy artist – purely neutral. Particular places too: Kweilin seemed touristy, but life also seemed charming. Perhaps most people there, not knowing how ugly it is somewhere else, don't realize how beautiful their place is. The beauty of it neutralizes it, from this point of view. Since our trip everybody I have met who had been to China, but had not visited Kweilin, said they wanted to go there. Some people have said, weren't you disappointed in Canton? But I wasn't at all. The difference between that city and Peking is interesting. In Peking, the walls, the hard, straight lines, everybody the same; whereas in Canton, the different faces, the hotter city, the amusement park which we were terrified of at first as Mr Lin had called it the Cultural Park. I was expecting it to be quite boring, people forced into roles, into listening to boring entertainment. And you felt Mr Lin was a bit ashamed of it until he realized we were fascinated by it. You can make patterns in different ways now. Madame Sun Yat-sen died while we were there. She was a neutral figure. So was the mourning for her, although an awful lot of people didn't seem to notice she'd died; and how respectful Mr Lin was about her. At first, we didn't quite know who she was; then we found out that her sister was Madame Chiang Kai-shek and that made you think she was probably an opportunist. And yet she might have been a dear, wonderful lady and a deep patriotic Chinese, which is what Mr Lin suggested she was.

Nanking seemed a neutral area: we were less aware there of being in a communist country: the prettiness of the boulevards and the trees and the activity of the streets, and when it rained, leaving all the streets fresh, that too seemed neutral. Shanghai seemed to go back to the communist world. The hotel was quite amusing. It is now called the Shanghai Mansions, written up in English outside, with no Chinese at all; full of English. It used to be called the Broadway Mansions. The people we talked to hanging around outside the hotel we knew were not representative of young Chinese; they were more aggressive, entrepreneurial, eager, curious, wanting to travel, people who in any other country would have got on a boat and gone off somewhere. If Londoners were trapped in London and could not leave, there'd be certain types who'd hang around West End hotels, full of foreigners, wanting news of the outside world.

SS And what about the beggars? I wrote a poem about a beggar in a country where there aren't supposed to be any beggars. That was in Canton. Beggars are non-persons too. In addition to the neutral, there's a sort of gap, a vacuum always in these countries, of people you're not supposed to look at, who are not supposed to exist at all.

DH Well, there are a lot of people that don't exist, officially! Let us now go through the people we got to know, mostly guides, in a kind of descending order; they've got to be brought to life. We have Mr Lin at the top. After Mr Lin, would you think the guide from Peking? She's a bit vague to me.

SS Well, I think we can type her in; she never speaks anything but statistics.

DH The guide in Sian was in love with the driver, she flirted with him. She didn't tell us anything, but it was nice to see that the driver of the car and she were more interested in each other than in us. Mr Lin thought that was terrible, but, frankly, I didn't. The guide in Wusih was the one we had lunch with, an elaborate lunch; who had been to America, to France.

SS He'd been to Greenville, North Carolina, buying machinery. An Australian on a tour had written three poems for him.

DH He was the first guide with whom we began to discuss China. We had three or four hours' conversation with him. Again, we didn't know much about him. He'd just got married, I think, because we'd been discussing marriage, one child to a family, etc. At times you got the impression he was quite sensitive and at other times you got the impression he was rather coldly bureaucratic. . . .

Then we went on the boat. He talked about meditating. He's the person we thought a bit queeny at first, if you saw him in San Francisco, but very efficient. He had a sense of duty; a thoughtful person, in a way. He talked about the monks with some sympathy for the idea of meditating, but then he rejected all religion out of hand and you reacted in some ways as I would have done. I would have thought, he's being bossy, suggesting that people should not feel anything about that sort of thing. He seemed to me like a very cool bureaucrat. He'd been to other countries, he'd seen what it was like there and he very consciously wanted to bring China up to their standard – though he thinks the Party will do this, but he's doing his bit and you get the idea he'd do anything to keep that idea going, including being a bit inhuman, at times.

The guide in Kweilin was the person we got to know best after Mr Lin. Also Mr Lin knew that, as he was the only guide about whom we talked to Mr Lin. When you talked to him, he never stumbled over what you said, over what anyone said, and he answered. He seemed closer to us. The last two were the guides in Canton, the girl and the man. They were both charming. We remember them because they were rather easy-going, much the least official people we came across, even less than the guide in Kweilin; life had taught them a few lessons, they were not quite as young and naive. The way the one was always jolly, always smiling, looked as though he enjoyed life, he always laughed at the jokes in English – as Mr Lin chose to laugh at some and not at others! Altogether, you see, there were only about four or five Chinese people with whom we made any real contact, all guides.

SS There was, of course, Mu-li, the artist in Peking, who did the picture of Mao on the horse; we made a good contact with him and he told us quite a lot; he was trying to put himself across quite hard.

DH He certainly was. Of all the people in that room, he put himself across more than anybody else. Partly because of the work, but also because his personality did. He was eager to go to England, and therefore he was eager to use his English, eager to speak with some English people. You know, if you were eager to learn a bit of French and some French people had come, you would be the one to talk to them.

Then, in descending order, there are other people: I remember the manager of the lacquer factory because I thought he looked exactly like Alfred Newman, a rather jolly character. And the professor in Kweilin whom we got to know a bit.

SS He had been through the Cultural Revolution; he'd been very badly mauled, he obviously was a rather crushed man. He didn't say anything which wasn't completely orthodox. When we discussed music he was completely on the puritanical line.

DH Do you think that was because Mr Lin was always there? After all, we all remember Mr Lin saying, I am higher than he is, he's just a professor; I'm a government official. He meant it, and the Professor knew that as well. What we don't know is whether he would relax when talking with us alone. Naturally, he might have felt he had to side with Mr Lin.

SS Do you think Mr Lin was doing a kind of tour of inspection of the guides we met?

DH When I spoke to him about the guide in Kweilin, how much we liked him, how excellent we thought his English was, how intelligent we thought he was, After our river trip Mr Lin arranged a dinner for the five of us at the hotel, a feast. Mr Lin wanted to impress him. He wasn't trying to impress us, he couldn't really, but I think the dinner was arranged to show us that he was high up and also because he knew we had talked to the guide without him being there and he wanted to put the boy in his place in some way. If three non-English-speaking Chinese came to Britain and couldn't read any signs, so they needed a guide constantly to show them round Britain, they would probably have a semi-government official, more than likely from the British Council, wouldn't they?

SS Yes, suppose we had been three Chinese poets, travelling round in England and we tried to put on a show of Chinese poetry at an English university, the English would have done much worse, wouldn't they?

DH But to go back to the subsidiary characters, the people we came across, whom else can we remember in Peking?

SS The poets. The woman poet whom we nicknamed Oilrig. She told us quite a bit about herself. She told us that she had been in the army and she'd worked with a crew on an oilrig. The poets combined having an official view of themselves with considerable candour just the same.

DH I thought the poetry was touching; it was interesting. At times, you wanted to laugh because of the strange sound that they made, although it was fascinating to know Chinese poetry was done in this way.

Other people we met: the boy out in the street in Sian who wanted the cigarettes.

SS He had a girlfriend who was on a bicycle and he wanted, having elicited money from us for the cigarettes, more money to buy a skirt for the girlfriend – which we didn't take up with any enthusiasm.

DH This is the point I'm making, though: none of the people in hotels did we get to know.

SS In Nanking, we visited the artists. Can you add anything to that?

DH I was feeling terrible then, I was green, I was beginning to think I'd go off back to Los Angeles. Who else did we meet in Nanking? A non-Chinese, the American lady. She struck us because she sat on her own in the dining room. She immediately started talking to us and told us that her husband was in the hospital; he loved Chinese food, he was mad about Chinese food, but there was too much salt in it which was bad for the heart; this was her theory. She was quite pleased with the Chinese doctors, and the nurses were good; the only thing that worried her was getting back to San Diego where they had a boat.

Then there was the little boy artist who is special because the only contact with him was through his art. It was a rare, wonderful day which we will not forget. In Hangchow we also met the artists at the lacquer factory whom we didn't know anything about, and when we left we still didn't know anything about them.

SS There were the houses they lived in that you liked so much. Do you remember? They had triangular fronts and people standing in the windows.

DH Hangchow was a beautiful place, a charming city and, the way we saw it, life seemed rather idyllic for a craftsman or an artist. You said you could teach there for six months. I could see that. It was a pretty town, the people all seemed very nice, if you got to know them, the young students in the art studio looked very eager; but we couldn't speak to them.

From Wusih we went to Shanghai by train. That was good because we had time to chat. We chatted quite a lot with Mr Lin. He told us a lot then: how, instead of being sent to Paris, they posted him to Reykjavik; then he went to Denmark. We talked a lot about the Cultural Revolution, what had happened; we tried to get his views on it. They were the currently official ones, that it was a great mistake. At the same time we were always asking him questions about the landscape.

In Shanghai the officials were dull. We went to the commune. The deputy director of the commune was a straightforward country person. I said to him, was it not insulting, really, to send townspeople to work in the country, which was like sending them to a prison, and he kind of agreed. He agreed because he thought the townspeople were no good on the land, they were useless; and when the officials came, they'd ask stupid questions. He seemed like a shrewd old peasant, like an old shrewd French peasant who despises the official who comes from Paris to tell him what to do, and he would treat him with a bit of contempt. The students we met in Shanghai, outside the hotel, we should assume were a bit out of the ordinary. First of all, they spoke English quite well, yet they were not officials. They were genuine students, studying science and other subjects, learning English, wanting to practise it and wanting to, obviously, express their complaints. They might represent something, but I wouldn't have thought they were absolutely representative. I think it would be very unfair to assume all Chinese youth were like that.

SS I think they probably *were* rather representative but of course we shouldn't assume so. You see, the Cultural Revolution started in Shanghai.

DH Yes, they were a certain bold type. One or two of them told us they had been Red Guards. One of them asked in a direct way about America, about England. They were aware that other countries were more affluent. I think the youth of Sian wouldn't be aware of that. We can assume they were young intellectuals with curiosity, wanting to meet people and know things. They asked where we had been in China, where we came from abroad and where we were going. They were interested in travelling. As a Red Guard you travelled about a lot of places. When Mr

Lin talked about the Cultural Revolution, he said how basically naive it had been to let loose all these kids on a free railroad. They roamed around. And you realize that any youngster might have become a Red Guard, exploring his country, people feeding him; there would have been millions. I don't think it was an ideological army at all; it was an army of adventurous teenagers. One of them said he was now about 26; so it was ten years before that he had been a Red Guard. We had thought that the Red Guards were a brainwashed, ideological army, when it obviously could have been nothing of the kind. The leaders would have been strongly ideological and the rest not.

SS But it doesn't explain the amazing violence.

DH Well, it was a mob. A mob can easily become violent. I think the violence would have come from the ideological leaders who were older, simply backed up by millions of teenagers. And remember that the teenagers would have been easily influenced by the leaders (and by Ch'in Ling in the background). You suddenly got a clearer picture of the naivete. When I had read about it in America I had got the impression that it was this marvellously trained group of people, disciplined. The violence would have come from the violent ideology of the leaders and the teenagers followed. The students we met in Shanghai were the first from the crowd to speak to us and complain.

Our mood kept changing: when we'd become convinced at one moment that it was a police state, the next day, we'd look around suspiciously for evidence and find it. The day after, the sun would shine on the lovely mountains of Kweilin

and you'd forget all about it and you'd enjoy the nature and the trees. That was a vivid part of the experience of being there. With our change of mood, the first person we looked at differently each time was Mr Lin. When he were convinced China was a police state, we saw Mr Lin as a bit of a monster; when we'd forgotten about it, Mr Lin was just the charming man that he appeared to us to be!...

We come now to our contrasts: the Stalinist idea and the traditional, to Canton. The rather sweet guide in Kweilin had said Canton was terrible, we wouldn't like it, a horrible city. I think that was the official line, like Mr Lin's was: he did not like Canton. It was like the official who lives outside Washington who would tell you New York is a sin city. Yet I thought Canton was very enjoyable, lively, the most lively city in China. The streets were full of people, they all looked a bit different, it was the only place we began to see girls in dresses, it was hotter as well, at night it seemed brighter, there were more restaurants. It was the only place where we actually saw people consciously going to a place to enjoy themselves, the so-called Culture Park. I think an official of the British Council, taking someone on a tour of England, if they'd finally got to Blackpool in August, would be a bit condescending about it: he'd say, Blackpool: a working-class fun city. In fact he wouldn't have grasped Blackpool's crude and vulgar pleasures, that the reason for its charm is its vulgarity. The very touching thing in Canton was when we discovered the Children's Park. We were passing and I saw something interesting, looking in and asked Mr Lin what was this place. He told us and we walked in. It all looked very beautiful and the first thing we saw were children sweeping up, keeping it tidy. There hardly seemed any adults at all, you didn't even have, like you might have done in England, the park keeper sitting around. The only ones were some mothers who were looking after the young ones. The little girl who followed us knew I was taking pictures, so she would run up the slide and slide down. She was pretty, in a nice green dress; I've got photographs of her. She was a little bit wanting to show off, and Mr Lin was very, very sweet to her and chatted to her and she seemed to like him. He was not playing the official, he was just the kind man. Children, after all, know whether someone is a kind person or an official; they're not fools. The park was a gem, beautiful, well kept, children keeping it clean, the little painted animals; it had an unbelievable innocence about it, more so than you would find here in L.A. The simplification of the forms of those animals: the chicken was done with a beautiful innocent form to it that was more innocent than, say, Mickey Mouse. When I got back to Hong Kong, I wrote a letter to Mr Lin thanking him and I said, 'I know you thought I wouldn't like Canton much, but I was more moved by the Children's Park in Canton than by all the monuments.' It was the most human part of China, the real people, like all human beings, brothers really, and it gave you that feeling. And it gave you it in a simple childlike way which the political way, trying to do something similar, does not.

A permanent problem in a socialist country is that after the heroic revolution, through which socialism has been established, everything is built on the *memory* of that event: you read about the Long March, Mao Tse-tung and whoever was there; it dominated their lives, coloured everything, more than their own childhood. When it happened, it must have been an adventure to all people in China. But for today's generation who did not experience it directly themselves, they only know because they're being told it was heroic. The swindle is that if you have to be told something that happened was heroic, it is not heroic in real terms, certainly not for you, in the way you feel.

SS This probably explains Mao's idea of having a continuous revolution and why he wanted to start the Cultural Revolution. Another point I wanted to make here was something Paul Theroux said to me, that China was not so much like school, as I suggested to him, but like the Boy Scouts, and Mao was the Chief Scout.

DH That's interesting, but is it true? One of the points about boy scoutism is that it's an attempt to give a sense of heroic adventure to the young. However, it's a bit false in that it's mock heroics; very few people would think it was *really* adventurous. It's just like the Outward Bound idea. Climbing the rock face under stress is obviously heroic in a corny way, but the fact is that you know what you're going into. It is certainly not like Mao on his march when you don't know what the result is going to be. And how do you convince people that it is a great, bold adventure worth having? It's not normal for ordinary people to want a big adventure. Most people would be happy just with the quiet 'adventure' of life, and to them all life is an adventure in that sense, but they want it quietly; other people do not, they want it heroically, they join up in armies, they are prepared to face violence in life.

But to make a whole nation feel heroically inclined like this is impossible unless a momentous event happens at one particular moment, like in 1949 when they took over. I'm sure the whole nation would have had a sense of its being heroic then. This sort of thing happens in times of war: Churchill gave the British people a sense of it. You could have put up with anything, lack of food, life changes; but the excitement of the struggle replaces other things. Just as in Russia, in 1917, where this heroic sense lasted until Stalin really got himself firmly in power. In the twenties and early thirties, it must have been a thrilling heroic time for most Russian people, all that genuinely revolutionary art they produced, among other things, the fact that they felt they'd taken over control. But in the end, it is watered down, in countries like that, where a strong ideology, the orthodoxy, takes over and the swindle comes in then, trying to pass on this heroic adventure as a permanent state that just is not true. The Poles suffer it now: the young want adventure, they're willing to sacrifice many things, they don't mind if there's no meat in the shops so long as they can take over their freedom. When they can't, then they complain about everything else. And yet, I'm sure it's true of some people when they say that they are fed up with Solidarity; they simply want a very quiet life. How do you convince the third or fourth generations that it's still a heroic struggle? In our part of the world we don't have to do that because many things are open to you, you always have a sense of things you can go forward to. And to talk of the good of China, the State, is such an abstracted adventure; you'd have to be like Lenin to grasp that strange abstraction. An ordinary person just wanting vigour can't grasp that. And to say that that is counter-revolutionary is no good. But it's no good dismissing the idea of adventure as though it were a sin. The whole history of the world is made up of people who set out on adventures and did things.

SS   There is a difficulty, however, with countries like Russia or China, where a revolution took place a generation or two ago, and the country continues to be run by the same old men who, when they were young, took part in that revolution (now a failing dream in their old minds). In those countries the adventurous alternative to their now reactionary society is the very form of society from which they originally 'saved' their nations by making the revolution – Capitalism. Which do we prefer? The People's Republic of China or Hong Kong?